A Misplaced Sense of Loyalty
-Marc Costello-

Copyright © 2020

Mayhem Books

The moral right of the author has been asserted.

All rights reserved.

Dedications & Acknowledgments

I would like to dedicate A Misplaced Sense of Loyalty to Danny Costello and Michael Costello. How I wish, how I wish you were here.

Also…
Terry Costello and Janet Costello. Thank you for your love and support over the years. I know at times I did not deserve it.

I would like to thank my wife Louise for the love, support and believing in me. I will always appreciate it.

Special thanks to fellow author Lance Manley for his guidance, cover design and editing of this book.

Front cover photo by AJ Gallagher on Unsplash.

Chapters

Chapter 1 – Strangers in the family

Chapter 2 – From dawn to dusk

Chapter 3 – Lost uniform with a bent arm

Chapter 4 – Down with the hippies

Chapter 5 – Early morning run ins

Chapter 6 – A storm is brewing

Chapter 7 – Four cans and a bottle of cider

Chapter 8 – A short sharp shock

Chapter 9 – 266 Costello, Sir!

Chapter 10 – The story of H.A.T

Chapter 11 – A trip to hell and back

Chapter 12 – Running riot with the Peel Street boys

Chapter 13 – On the merry go round

Chapter 14 – A pair of trainers, a game of pool and a cream bun

Chapter 15 – Sheep dogs to crown court trials

Chapter 16 – Justice on the strand

Chapter 17 – A sweet smell of sorrow

Chapter 18 – And then there were three

Epilogue

Chapter 1 – Strangers in the Family

When people look back on their life, they try not to have too many regrets. I am someone who is like that, but I do have regrets and my biggest one is what I put my family through.

The thing is that I had a good childhood with loving parents and two younger brothers. We had a nice home, did not want for much and yet there I was, hellbent on throwing it all away and for what? Thirty plus years later I am still asking myself that same question and hopefully, after writing this book I can find out the answer and work out where it all went wrong.

I was born Marc Lee Costello in January 1973 at West Park hospital in Macclesfield, an old silk town in Cheshire. I was named after Marc Bolan from the band T-Rex. They were riding high in the charts at the time and were one of the biggest bands in the UK. Mum and dad have always been big music lovers and they both enjoyed going to gigs and seeing all the great bands from that era. This meant that me and my brothers were all brought up listening to good music.

We set up home on the Hurdsfield Estate which, at the time, was the best estate in Macclesfield. In 2020 the community spirit is not there anymore, and it has totally changed, like most estates in different towns and cities across England. However, I have nothing but fond memories of living there.

Two years later in 1975 my brother Terry was born. Not in hospital like me but at home and a couple of years later we moved a couple of minutes away, on the other side of the Hurdsfield Junior school, which I attended.

I don't really remember much about living at my first house apart from mum telling me that I could never stay still. I was always trying to escape from the house and on many occasions when mum's back was turned, I would be off with my nappy dragging behind me. There was a time when I got lost in Blackpool, apparently. I just wandered off down the promenade without a care in the world.

My mum and dad were frantic with worry looking for me. A policeman found me and brought me back.

My first strong memories are from the second home. We had a big orchard at the back of our house and together with the kids from our road we would all go off and spend hours in there, building dens and climbing trees. We would collect apples and someone's parents would bake apple pies for us to share.

When other kids came in there to play, they would get lost but we knew every little pathway between the shoots that were growing there. One time we were playing in the orchard when Terry got stuck up a tree. He was shouting for help so instead of going to get my dad I ran to the phone box and rang the fire brigade who, to everyone's embarrassment, came and rescued Terry and took him home to his mum and dad who weren't best pleased that I had rung 999.

For years, every Guy Fawkes night all the adults and us kids would build a bonfire in the orchard. Everyone would club together and chip in for food and drink and we would all gather around together, watching the fireworks. It was a real sense of community, everyone looking out for each other.

As kids growing up on our road, the main thing I remember was that we would always be in and out of each other's houses. The doors were always unlocked, we were welcome to come and go as we pleased. This community spirit became evident when a man called Don Harper announced that he had purchased the orchard and was going to flatten it and build houses on there instead. We were outraged by this because this was where we played, and we didn't want it to happen so everyone got together and we had demonstrations organised by my mum and dad and their friends. It got very heated and tempers were getting frayed especially when Don Harper wanted to cut a tree down, that was growing from our back garden and overhanging his property. Unfortunately, Harper Developments won, and the orchard was no more.

I attended Hurdsfield Infant School and then later Hurdsfield Junior, both of which were just around the corner from our house. I enjoyed school and became popular, making lots of friends, some of which I still know to this day. I was part of the school football team and I remember after one game when I was about 10, in the presentation party was Alex Williams, Manchester City goalkeeper at the time. We didn't win but I remember there was a couple of Manchester United players as well, but I can't remember which ones.

Playing football became a big part of my life and around this time my dad and my mum's brother Jimmy were doing discos together in the local clubs and stuff like weddings, anywhere really that would book them.

They named their disco Marc Lee Productions after me and I remember they wrote it in marker pen on the box that contained all their 7-inch singles. My dad was always out doing the discos when he could. On weekend nights, me and Terry would help him, carrying the gear that he had hired from a shop in Macclesfield called Vampire Acoustics.

My dad worked as a scaffolder. He always worked every hour that god sent to provide for his family. My mum worked as a nurse at Parkside which was a hospital for mental health but, like many other old buildings, it was demolished, and houses and apartments have replaced it.

On these Saturday nights mum and dad would get a babysitter for me and Terry and they would then go out together with either dad or my uncle Jimmy doing the discos. It meant that mum was enjoying the night out as well.

One story that dad told me were that he was the DJ at Ian Curtis's wedding reception. Ian Curtis, for those who don't know, was the lead singer in the band Joy Division who very sadly killed himself on the eve of the band's first American tour. Ian used to knock around with my uncle Jimmy and my mum's cousin Pat and he also knew my dad. A few years later my dad was DJ-ing at a disco and Ian was there. He asked my dad if he would play this record that he had on him. It was a first pressing of Joy Division's new single Love Will Tear Us Apart. When the song had finished, he then handed it back to Ian, who told my dad he could have it, but my dad refused, saying he didn't like it leaving Ian stood there. I can imagine what that would be worth now. Never mind, that is what my dad was like.

What I remember the most about these times, is spending all my time around my nana Naden's house, which was only around the corner. In fact, both my mum's and dad's parents lived near to us at one time or another. If we called round there you could be guaranteed that my nana would make us a jam butty. Every time, it was all she would make us. She always made the most burned toast you had ever seen as well. She would eat the toast and drink cups of tea that were stewed in an old teapot.

My dad's parents both came from Ireland. My grandad was from County Mayo in southern Ireland and my nana was from Warrenpoint which is in the north, which in itself was a strange set up, especially in those days with the different divisions that separated the two areas. They came over to England and settled in Salford just outside Manchester where my grandad got a job as a groundworker. My dad was born in Salford in January 1951, the eldest of five with four of them boys.

When me and Terry called round to nana Costello's house, we would go into the back garden and pick the apples from the tree that was growing there. My nana would then make us apple pies that we would share between our friends. The good thing about being around my nana Costello's house, was that the school field backed onto her garden, so we would hop over the fence and play football until it went dark and we had to go home. Thinking about these times it has struck me that no one could ever understand a word that my grandad said. He had the strongest Irish accent that, to this day, I have ever heard. I can't really remember having a conversation with him, but I must of because he was my grandad, but they were few and far between that's for sure.

My grandad Costello loved a drink and after a hard day at work he would always be in his local pub, The Mulberry Bush, which was round the corner, drinking with his friends. I always remember a funny story about him when he had bought himself some new work boots and after a couple of days of wearing them, he started complaining they were killing his feet. They were really hurting him. Anyway, someone said to him 'take them off and let us have a look' which my grandad did. His friend then started laughing really hard and pointed out that my grandad had been wearing the boots on the wrong feet.

It seems strange writing about this almost forty years later, remembering when my brother Danny was born in 1981. Later there was a massive rift between Danny and my nana that has never healed.

No one seems close at all on my dad's side. It was a totally different setup to how things were on my mum's side. I was always close to my grandparents on my mum's side. Over the years it seems like we have become strangers to each other which is sad. My uncle Frank had it tough with his wife Janet over the last few years, but it is good to see them both in a good place.

Me and my uncle Tony had a falling out a few years ago. Things were said that I wish were not said and I regret that. When I was young, I used to spend a lot of time with Tony. Me and Terry used to go camping with him all the time. He used to take us camping at Wincle in the countryside. We would set up camp and we would go and get wood to build a fire, He would take us rock climbing as well. He took us to London so we could attend a CND rally. We had some great times with him growing up. When Tony moved to the Isle of Wight, in the school holidays I would travel on the train with my nana and we would spend a couple of weeks on the island at Tony's house. We never saw that much of him in the later years because he spent a lot of time in France where he bought a house that he tried to renovate.

With the breakup of my marriage to my first wife it was time to leave the family home. Tony found me and invited me to stay at his, which is what I did until it was time to move on and get my own place. It was round about this time that we started arguing, I felt that Tony was condescending towards me. He was always having a go at how I was being or how I was talking to someone and be fair he was probably right. I was in a bad place at the time. I was drinking a lot and felt that he didn't have the right to go on at me. So, we had words and I said a lot of bad things to him that I regret. I wish I had respected what he was saying instead of thinking "who the fuck does he think he is?!" and I'm sorry about that because he was there for me when I needed him.

Mum has two brothers, Jimmy and Roy, who we were close to growing up. More so Jimmy than Roy and I would see more of my uncle Jim because he did the discos with my dad and he was close to my mum. He died in 2009 after losing a short battle with cancer that devastated our family, especially my mum. I feel for my mum after everything she has been through, she has had a lot of tough times. I sometimes wonder how she has got through it all.

Roy is an incredibly talented artist who has painted some good pictures. Some years ago, he had an exhibition to showcase his paintings at Macclesfield Library, where he sold a few. He's a hairdresser by trade who used to work in some of the salons in town. He has a son, my cousin Terry, who was affectionately known during his early years as Terry 2.

I am the eldest in all of my family including my brothers and all my cousins, I have different relationships with them all. Some of them I see about, others that I don't see at all. We are family and

I wish them and their families well and I am there for them.

I was always in my nana's company. If I fell over then it wasn't my mum that I wanted, it was my nana Naden. She would come round to see to me. The good thing was she only lived around the corner near the launderette. Mum worked in their part time so while she was doing her shift, I was happy as Larry at my nana's house.

I have such happy memories from this time with my nana and grandad I couldn't wait to be around them. I just feel sad looking back about the hurt I caused them through my actions, especially my nana but I will get to that later. My grandad used to take me rabbiting up in the Hollins near the golf course overlooking Macclesfield. We used to go up there at night, digging some holes and setting up the nets and then we went home and waited for the following morning when we would go back to see if we had caught any. Any that we caught, my grandad would kill them, and I would bag them up. We would take these back to my grandad's cellar and hang them up. My grandad would then skin a couple and we would give them to my nana, who would cook us all rabbit pie for our tea. I loved these times, spending time with my grandad, he would also take me fishing on the canal. That was until the time I fell in.

We had arranged to go fishing the following morning and with it being an early start I was sleeping over at my nana and grandad's house. We got up at 5am and had some breakfast and my nana gave us a flask of coffee and some sandwiches that would last us the day. We soon arrived at the canal, it was a foggy morning with dawn breaking and mist rising over the water. We started unloading the car and before long my grandad was getting me ready to cast in. After about a minute I decided that I wasn't happy with the cast and wanted to change my location, so I started reeling my line back in. Grandad asked me what I was doing, so I said I wanted to get nearer to the other side so I was changing my peg, He told me to sit down where I was and fish from there. There was a barge next to where we were fishing so I climbed on to the barge with the rod in my hand. Grandad was going mad at this point telling me to get off the boat and sit back down. Well, I knew what was best and I ignored him. I stood near to the edge of the barge, swung my arm back and I let go of the line. I then slipped on the barge and at this point I flew headfirst straight into the canal with my rod landing with me in the freezing cold morning. I scrambled to the bank where my grandad pulled me out on to the grass verge. I sat there soaking wet and freezing cold with my grandad going mad at me, whilst he packed all the fishing stuff away telling me he would never take me fishing again. It's funny looking back on this story because he never even set up his rod or had a mouthful of coffee from his flask when I went flying into the canal. We hadn't been there twenty minutes before he was taking me back home for a warm bath.

When I got a bit older, I would meet him at Macclesfield bus station, and we would go up to South Park and play on the 9-hole golf course. We would play up there regularly and when I walk through there now, I look back on these times with a smile on my face.

My favourite times were when I would sleep over at their house. We would stay up late and watch Match of the Day with Jimmy Hill, the presenter at the time. Then I would get onto a camp bed that was made up for me at the bottom of their bed. Happy times and great memories. It was around this time that my grandad used to take me to watch our local side Macclesfield Town, who were playing in the Northern Premier league. The crowds were low, but I loved it, going up there with my grandad. We never missed a home game for years during this time. I remember on one occasion on a cold foggy midweek night, watching Macclesfield against Gainsborough Trinity and the official attendance was twelve but even that was generous. It felt like it was just me and my grandad there. We used to stand on the grass banking behind the goal on the Star Lane end. When the ball came over, me and the other kids would run and try and get it, so we could kick it back to the players. My grandad caught it once and passed it to me, so I could throw it back. It made me feel dead chuffed and I was buzzing.

Behind the grass banking was a five-a-side pitch that we sometimes played on at half time or during the game if it were boring, until the stewards locked the gates so we couldn't play there anymore. A few years later I used to train there when I played for Bollington Juniors and we used to go on the pitch taking penalties at the Star Lane end until we got shouted and told to get off the pitch. Many years later I streaked on the pitch during Macclesfield's last game in the conference against Bromsgrove. It was the last home game before they got promoted into the football league for the very first time. The streak I did is something I still get reminded of to this day. At the time it was a laugh but now I feel embarrassed but hey ho, I did it and it gave everyone there that day a good laugh and something to remember.

I think I was about 11 when my grandad Costello passed away. My nana Costello died a few years ago but I hadn't spoken to her for about fifteen years. I will go into detail later in the book why I never went to her funeral and I feel sad looking back and maybe I should have made an effort and let bygones be bygones and made my peace with her but I didn't. None of my family did and it's a shame.

Chapter 2 - From Dawn to Dusk

Growing up living on the Hurdsfield estate during the 70s and 80s was an enjoyable time, me and my friends would play out from dawn to dusk.

If we weren't playing in the orchard behind our houses, we would be on the school field playing football or cricket with the other kids from the estate. We only stopped when it was time to call it a night mum or dad would come to the top of the banking where the school fence is and shout us to come home. Even then we would argue for an extra five minutes or to play 'the next goal is the winner'.

Summers were hot in those days and we would spend our time walking in the hills, playing up there or heading to Rainbow Park which had a stream nearby. Sometimes if my dad wasn't working and the weather was good, he would take us up to Hurdsfield reservoir, where my dad and my uncles would put a rope swing up so we would take it in turns being pushed. Sometimes we would let go and dive in and swim around without a care in the world.

Mum used to hate us going up there, she used to argue with my dad saying it was dangerous and we could drown, but me and Terry would back dad up because we loved the place. All our friends would be there, and we didn't want to miss out and, in the end, mum used to come with us. Even though she hated it, she would sit and watch and enjoy the sun. Everyone from the estate would be up there. It's madness when you look back, because I wouldn't dream of doing it now, but in them days it was so normal.

One day I was up there with Terry and my dad and uncle Frank and Tony. We had been for a walk with my nana Costello's dog Mitzi and were walking back when Mitzi ran past me and knocked me into the water. I could hardly swim at this point, I must have been about six or seven years old and I was under the water panicking, when my dad scooped me out, The problem now was that I was soaking wet and if we went home like this mum would go mad at my dad for letting this happen even though it was an accident. Tony suggested we build a fire so we could dry my clothes off, so that is what we did. Then we returned home with mum none the wiser after my little swim. I can even remember the Scotland football top I had on from the world cup in 1978.

Those days seem a lifetime ago which, in a way they were, but they were magical times, when life was simple. We, as a family, didn't have much but everyone was in the same boat. My mum and dad worked hard to provide for me and my brothers and we made do with what we had. It was a close-knit community on our estate, everyone got on well with each other and looked out for others. There is nothing like that now which is a shame.

When I was old enough, I joined the 1st Hurdsfield Cub Scouts. my next-door neighbours Clive and Ian were already in the cubs, so we would walk down together to the scout hut. My dad used to do discos on a Saturday night at the scout hut and there were also jumble that took place on a Saturday afternoon. We would go round and collect bags that people had donated and would then take it to the scout hut where it would be sorted out. We would get a chance to buy something before the doors opened and when they did it would be like a free-for-all with everyone fighting for the best bargains. Many a time us kids would be walking around the estate in someone else's old jumper or T-shirt that there mums had donated, we weren't bothered where it came from, everyone was the same so it didn't matter.

We would go on camping trips to Barnwood scout camp at Rushton and we would pitch the big tents that slept about six of us at a time. Other cub and scout groups from around the Macclesfield and Cheshire area would also camp there. There were plenty of activities for us all to get involved in like canoeing where I learnt how to capsize and escape. I then progressed onto doing an Eskimo roll and we had great fun lining the canoes up and running over them till we fell off and into the river. I went to the Lake District with the scouts and we camped at Lake Windermere and spent hours canoeing. We canoed the width of the lake and then the more experienced scouts canoed from one end of the lake to the other, ending up in Ambleside where those who weren't involved went in the back of the scout bus and met up with them at the end of the trip.

There was a community centre on our estate that was an active place. On Monday nights a man who lived on our road ran a karate group. We all joined and gave it a go, but to be fair I didn't last long. It wasn't for me and I soon lost interest. There was also a youth club that was run from the community centre. We would go there and play pool or table tennis and get drinks and sweets from the tuck shop. It also used to have bingo nights and sometimes discos and we would help by putting the chairs out for the old ladies that played bingo.

The community centre was a busy place with something going on there most nights, especially during the 1980s and going into the 90s. About fifteen years ago it closed down for good and sadly it ended up being left to go to ruin, a proper eyesore for everyone to see until it was pulled down and houses were built there in its place. There seems to be no call for community centres anymore, I think that's wrong because it was somewhere to go for the kids. Instead of roaming the streets getting into trouble they could go there and play pool and whatever. Now that's gone what is there for the youth of our next generations?

I was playing a lot of football and ended up playing for the junior school team. I remember the night before my first game, we took our strips home because the game was on the following Saturday morning. I was in bed but couldn't sleep with excitement. Our school strip was the old West Bromwich Albion away one, green and yellow. I couldn't wait to put it on and get out there and I can't remember who we played or what the score was but I remember in the morning, myself and Clive my next-door neighbour, were on the school field about two hours before kick-off in our strips playing. That was until the schoolteacher came running over asking us what we were playing at.

It is funny that I remember the strips that we used to wear. This was late 70s early 80s when kits were becoming fashionable. I played for Hurdsfield Reds which was run by a great man called George Penn. We played on Vicky Park where the flats were. We were playing a lot of football on the school field from morning through to the night. Rain or shine, we were never in the house. If there were enough people, we would have a match, picking sides depending on the numbers. Either way we would be kicking a ball, pretending we were at Wembley and trying to win the pretend tournament.

Our Terry wasn't interested in football at this point, he didn't really get involved. He preferred to play with his Action Man or Star Wars figures. It wasn't his game which is surprising because he turned out to be a very good footballer. A little time later Terry played for the cubs with me. I was Centre Forward, terry used to play in midfield. I would be scoring goals for fun but Terry just couldn't score no matter how easy the chance was for him, so I would go around the keeper to make an open goal but instead of scoring into the empty net, I would always try to set Terry up. Unfortunately, he would miss and the chance would be go begging and I would have Tommy shouting at me to score instead of passing, but I persevered and Terry finally got one off the mark.

One day I was playing football on the school playground with my best mate Johnny. We were just kicking the ball at the wall it went on to the school roof. Now this would happen most times when we played on the school playground and what would usually happen is the one who kicked it up had to climb up the drain pipe and onto the school roof to retrieve the ball. Just as I was about to climb up my dad shouted me telling me I had to come home. Johnny said not to worry he'd get it, so off I went thinking nothing more of it.

Later on, that night I was woken up by my mum. The police were there and it turned out Johnny hadn't returned home from playing out. It was late so his parents had reported him missing. With me being the last one to see him they wanted to know where I had left him and if I knew where he could be. I told them that I had kicked the ball on the roof and Johnny said he was going to get it and then he was going to go home. The police asked me to get dressed and show them exactly where this was, so we went back to the school playground where I showed them what had happened and where we used to climb up onto the roof. The fire brigade was called and they spotted a broken skylight and that's where they found Johnny. He had fallen through the skylight and was lying unconscious in the caretaker's office. He was taken to hospital where he stayed until he was well enough to come back home.

Johnny was my best friend and we were inseparable, always trying to outdo each other, and would take penalties at each other for hours at a time, until one of us would say the other was better but we never would give in. Years later when we were both playing in the same Sunday league team, we used to argue like mad on who would be the penalty taker. We would toss a coin with whoever won taking the penalties until they missed one and at that point the other would take over.

We also used to pretend we were DJs in his bedroom. We would record us talking to each other as though we were doing made up interviews. We would be playing records from compilations like Now That's What I Call Music 10 and would tape the Top 40 and play that, pretending we were the famous DJs.

After Johnny's accident there was a change in him. He was more aggressive and argumentative and would storm off if he were getting beaten at anything but half an hour later it would be forgotten and we would continue playing like nothing had happened. Looking back, there may have been a lack of oxygen that starved his brain when he was lying in the caretaker's office that altered his personality. I don't know if that did happen but very sadly, in 2013 he took his own life and his loss affected a lot of people because he was an extremely popular lad who everyone liked and loved. I will never forget him. You were a legend my friend.

Chapter 3 – Lost Uniforms with a Bent Arm

In September 1984 I started secondary school. I was hoping to go to Macclesfield High where most of my mates were going but my mum thought it would be better if I went to Tytherington High. I argued my case saying that I did not want to go, but in the end my parents decided that was where I would be going and that was that. Hurdsfield Juniors historically always sent their pupils to Macc High, so I had expected to go there as well.

Now, with me going to Tytherington it meant that I would have to make new friends, not that it would be a problem as I got on well with most people and there were a few coming with me from my old school, but we were second class in a way. There were big houses in Tytherington but Hurdsfield was a council estate so there was a stigma there straight away. At Macclesfield High you didn't have that problem because everyone came from the estate or they came from the neighbouring Victoria flats so everyone was the same. Tytherington was always posher, with the purple blazers and grey trousers and we knew that.

When you went to a new school, the first thing that your mum had to do was to go and buy new school uniform. There was a shop in Macclesfield town centre called Scoltex, where everyone went no matter which school you were attending. So, off me and my mum went with a list of things that we needed. The trouble with this shop was they had the monopoly and it was expensive because everything had to be official. Tytherington's uniform was purple and Macc High's was dark blue and so on. This was the only place you could buy what you needed so my parents had to save up to get me it all.

After getting measured up and fitted out, my mum and I were walking out with a couple of bags containing my school uniform and went to Tesco's so mum could do a bit of shopping before we got a taxi home. When mum was at the checkout, she told me to wait near the cigarette kiosk and when walked out of the store and got into a cab, this is where disaster struck.

We got home, carried the bags into the house and mum asked me where my uniform was. My heart sank with the realisation that I didn't have the bags with me. Mum asked me again and at this point I started to cry as it suddenly dawned on me that I had left them in Tesco's. When I said this to my mum she went berserk. I had never seen her so angry. She was shouting and I knew it was my fault and I was in trouble. I wasn't hanging about with mum really mad at me so I legged it out of the house and didn't stop running until I had reached Tesco's where I prayed that my uniform had been handed in but no one had seen it. I couldn't believe it. I didn't know what to do but knew that I couldn't face my mum. She was so upset because the school uniform had cost a fortune, money that my parents could not afford in the first place, never mind having to fork out the same again because of my stupidity. Someone had found that uniform and kept it, so if you're reading this just think of that poor boy crying in the middle of Tesco's.

The next thing I know is my dad turned up and came over to see if I was alright and told me not to worry. He then spoke to the store manager to see if anything could be done but there was nothing more the store manager could do except contact us if it was handed in.

We returned home and my mum had calmed down a bit but she had been crying because she knew that we had no money to replace the uniform and she did not know what to do. My Nana Naden came to the rescue. She told my grandma about what had happened and after hearing this she gave mum the money to replace everything which we were all extremely grateful for.

I soon settled in, making new friends both in and out of school, some of which would become lifelong. I was still playing football after school on the school field, and also spending time playing with my friends, going around their houses for tea and having sleepovers. At night we would go out hedge hopping. This consisted of jumping over someone's hedge whilst trying not to make too much noise making sure the homeowner wouldn't hear us, because if we were heard they would come out to have a go at us. We would fly through these gardens one after another getting more and more adventurous all the time and knowing full well, we were asking for trouble. The amount of bollockings we used to get was rising daily but we just carried on thinking nothing of it. Some of the hedges were a mess after we had finished with them but we were young and having fun. We certainly didn't mean any harm but looking back at what we were doing you wouldn't get away with it now. There would be an outcry at the state some of those hedges were left in after we had charged through them. We were basically causing criminal damage to people's property but luckily it never went too far and a telling off was usually the end of the matter.

We soon progressed to garden sneaking, starting at one house then climbing into their back garden. We would then try and make our way through as many gardens as we could until we got to the end of the run. The downside to this game was if we were a few gardens in and there was no way of continuing, we would then have to go back the way we came. What made this more challenging was the fact that we would be doing this between seven and eight o'clock at night, when most people would be in their kitchens or living rooms. Any noises that we made, they would look out of the windows or open the back doors to see what was going on and we would be hiding in the back garden trying to keep still until they went back inside.

There were two main garden sneaks that we would attempt with one on Nicholson Avenue and the other on Brocklehurst Avenue, both around the corner from where I lived. The first one was the hardest and every kid on the estate must have had a go at doing this at one time or another. It was challenging due to the fact that it was uphill and this route had plenty of fences and hedges separating the gardens.

We had plenty of attempts until finally we would complete the sneak and then we would then boast to the other kids that we had completed the run to see if they could match us. It wasn't all plain sailing though, there were a few times in which we would get caught. We would be then be escorted out to the front with a word in our ear about telling our parents if they caught us again.

In reality now if this happened, they would ring the police and you would be arrested and possibly charged with attempted burglary. Back then there was nothing like that, thank god. We were just kids having fun with no malice.

After I had been in the cubs for a while, I was old enough to progress to the scouts and this also took place at the scout hut on a Thursday night.

The scouts had organised a trip to Alton Towers. I went with my next door neighbour Clive and we were both looking forward to it because, if I remember, this was the first time I had been to Alton Towers. I had heard about the rides there so I couldn't wait to have a go on the famous Corkscrew and the Black Hole.

We set off early, arriving in good time to enjoy the day. Things went well and soon it was time to head back to the arranged meeting point. It was then we realised that we were missing one lad. The scout leader gave him fifteen more minutes to turn up, but there was still no sign of him and everyone was getting a bit worried. It was decided that we would split up in to twos and go round the park looking for him and report back to the meeting point in half an hour. So off me and Clive went and we hadn't got very far when we decided to have another go on one of the rides. We saw there was no queue for a ride called the Octopus, so we both jumped on and enjoyed a last go. Unfortunately for me it so nearly was my last ever ride.

We both got on and were enjoying ourselves, and after a couple of minutes, with the ride going up and down I noticed the lad who we were supposed to be looking for. Me and Clive started shouting at him but he couldn't hear us due to the noise so in my wisdom I decided when the ride started slowing down that I would jump off. What actually happened was the ride slowed down, I climbed out of my seat then I tried to jump but as I did, I caught my arm on the bar and it dragged me underneath the carriage, ragging me about as it was slowing down. At this point the emergency stop button was activated and the ride came to a halt.

I was in a lot of pain, I felt really dizzy like I was going to collapse and my left arm was looking like a U-shape where it was drooping down. The bones had been shattered, and I was in shock. The first aiders came to me straight away, and tried to make me as comfortable as they could, but it was obvious that I needed to get to hospital. It was not long before I could hear the sirens from the ambulance, and I was on my way to the North Staffordshire Hospital.

My mum and dad had been informed by the scout leader and they were soon on their way down to meet me. When they arrived, I was lying on a trolly waiting to be seen by a doctor. I was in pain and needed something to help me stay calm.

A doctor explained that they were waiting to X-ray me to see the extent of the damage. I was in agony so I was given gas and air to help with the pain as they tried to keep me calm. I was then wheeled into the X-ray department and had my arm scanned. When the doctor got the results, he could see that it was a bad break and I was going to need an operation to reset my arm. They did it later that afternoon and after a couple of days I was able to return home with a cast feeling sorry for myself.

The lad who we had been looking for came around to my house with his parents to see how I was. He wanted to apologise for not being at the meeting point but it wasn't his fault it was mine. I shouldn't have been on that ride; I should have been looking for the lad like we were told to. Even now if you look at my left arm it is different to my right because there is now a dip where it couldn't be fully straightened. A lasting reminder of my first trip to Alton Towers.

Chapter 4 – Down With The Hippies

I left school with no qualifications much to the disappointment of my parents as they had hopes and dreams for me, as any parent would have for their children. The amount of times I heard the words "You've got a brain why don't you use it?!" and they were right. My dad didn't want me following him into his line of work. He was a scaffolder and he wanted a better life for me. He knew it was a hard job as he worked long hours, seven days a week. He didn't want me to go down that same road working so hard just to bring a good wage home.

He wanted me to knuckle down, study hard at school and get some decent grades that would get me a good start in the real world. As ever and not for the first time I didn't listen to him. I enjoyed my school days; especially High school and I hardly ever missed a day. To be honest I never twagged school that much because I simply enjoyed going. Being with my mates and having a laugh, that was much better than staying at home or roaming the streets like the others did. I was popular, so that meant that I was becoming a jack-the-lad. I was always the first to get up to a bit of mischief in school and it was all harmless fun but it meant I was getting in trouble for disrupting the class and my parents weren't happy about that.

I used to walk to school with a friend who lived around the corner from me called Gareth. We were in the same class and we became good friends, but Gareth came from St John's School in Bollington where his dad was the headmaster and he was under pressure to do well, with high expectations placed on his shoulders but that never stopped him from having fun. We used to knock-on for another lad called Nick who lived near us and then go over the fields, then onto the old railway line and up the banking, over the school fence coming in the back entrance through the pine trees down onto the gravel where the hockey pitches were.

Near to the old railway line was a stream that ran under the bridge into the river Bollin and that was our playground. We would head there after school spending hours jumping the stream trying to see who could jump the furthest, daring each other to do crazier jumps until we would land too short and get soaked wet through. It was riskier after it had been raining and the stream was overflowing, not that it would stop us, it just added to the fun and you could guarantee we would all walk home with our school uniforms wet, knowing we had to face the inevitable bollockings that we would get when we returned home. Yet again our uniforms would have to be washed and dried for the following morning.

Once we were playing down the stream and it was after my accident at Alton Towers. My arm was still in its cast but that wasn't going to stop me from going down the stream and playing with my mates. I had every intention of not getting involved but soon I was dragged into the fray. They were having fun and the urge to join in was too much to resist. I waited for my turn and ran and that's when I slipped and fell into the stream with my cast going under the water. I stood up and fell back down then got to my feet and I knew I was in the shit. I was stood in the stream absolutely soaked wet through and to top it all, with my arm in a plaster cast that was now going all soggy and peeling off. I was cold and wet and trying to climb out of the stream but I couldn't. I kept falling back in and the more I was screaming to my mates to help me, the more they were rolling around crying with laughter. I finally got out and started making the slow walk home to face the music.

My arm was hurting. Most of the plaster cast had fallen off and I knew I was in trouble. I arrived home, mum took one look at the state of me and what was left of the cast. To say my mum and dad went ballistic is an understatement. After a change of clothes, I was off up to A&E to get a new cast and returned home to face the news that I was banned from going down the stream for a while.

We used to ride our bikes down to the coal yard at the end of the old railway line, which is where the big Tesco now stands. We built a track with some jumps out of the coal and took turns trying to master new move. This was until the bigger lads from the Vicky flats came along with their newer BMX's and took it over, meaning we would have to wait from a distance until they got bored so we could get back on there.

A couple of years later, one of my mate's dads bought him a Honda bog seat 90 cc motorbike. We used to ride this up and down the old railway line from the coal yard all the way as far as Bollington. We would take it in turns flying up and down having great fun, giving each other backeys. Looking back, we used to have some great times messing about down there. We were never bored, always making use of the day. Not like kids nowadays who moan if they are told to play out instead of being on their games consoles all the time.

Behind Hurdsfield church was Trinny fields, and we would knock around in there sometimes. The fields led to a little stream in Bluebell woods. We wouldn't venture too far in there because it was private property. Old man Bailey was the farmer who owned the land and if he saw us, he would shout and end up chasing us away. On the other side of the fields there was a big tree that someone had made a rope swing on and we would spend hours playing on it. I went back there recently to reminisce but you can't access the fields anymore and there is a sign up saying private property trespassers will be shot etc. When we played in there you would hear stories of local kids getting chased by old man Bailey with his gun. I never saw him with one but you never knew if it was true or not. If we had seen that sign in those days, we would have laughed at it and carried on, with the innocence of youth.

When I was about 11 or 12, BMX Bikes were becoming the next big thing in England. The bikes had originated from America, with the craze reaching these shores and now everyone was after one. The first bike that I remember having was a Raleigh Grifter a right lump of a bike. It was really heavy on the front end so you couldn't pull wheelies or do any tricks on it. The truth was it was built like a tank and weighed about the same. So, when people started riding around on their BMXs I knew I wanted one as well. I managed to talk my parents into getting me a BMX for my birthday. It wasn't brand new because we could never afford a new one but that never bothered me. It wasn't a Mongoose or a Diamond Back, it didn't have the Skyway wheels or anything like that, it was just a standard second-hand BMX and I was made up with it. I used to ride it everywhere, trying to learn all the tricks but most of the time just making it up as I went along.

The older kids from the estate had built a quarter pipe out of old creates and pieces of wood down at Banbury park. I used to go down there and watch them learning 360s and other fancy moves that they were practicing. I would be there waiting patiently for one of them to give me the nod so I could have a quick go.

It was also about this time that people were getting into breakdancing and soon everyone was walking around the streets with a roll of lino and some of their mum's furniture polish to keep it shiny for them to do their spins on. Our Terry was well into this as he could do the windmill, backspins, the lot with his little gang of breakdancers, whereas I was lucky to be able to do a head spin. It wasn't my scene but I enjoyed watching them do their moves and it was quite funny.

My Dad was still doing the discos at the scout hut. Every Saturday night everyone used to end up in a circle with a group of body poppers on one side, and another group opposite. There would be a burnout between the two groups to see who the best was. Dad would have to buy the latest Beat street records or Chaka Khan's new one to try to keep up with this new music that was around. Most of the kids had bought their own 12-inch records for my dad to play. It reminded me of when I went to the junior school discos and we would be allowed to take a couple of singles that I owned. I would give them to the DJ to be played and we had to put our names on our records so we could get them back. I used to take my Jam singles Going Underground and Beat Surrender. I was strutting around thinking I was Jimmy out of Quadrophenia but without the scooter.

Music has always been a massive part of my life; my parents always had an album playing on their stereo whenever they could. They would listen to music instead of watching TV, so it was always going to rub off on me. They were both massive Pink Floyd fans, buying all their albums, going to see them in concert at places like the Bingley hall in Stafford and in Manchester at the Free Trade hall in the 70s and 80s. One day my dad was giving me and my mates a lift up to Rainow. We were driving along and my dad was playing Pink Floyd's new album The Wall full blast on the car stereo. My mates were loving it and so was I. Still to this day when I hear the words "Daddy's flown across the ocean Leaving just a memory" I always remember back to that sunny day. Me with my mates on our way up to Rainow to play football in my dad's old Ford Cortina, and it makes me smile.

Every year in June mum and dad, along with my uncles, made the journey to the Glastonbury festival. Me, Terry and Danny used to stay at my Nana Naden's whilst they were there. In 1984 me and Terry went with them for the first time. We all climbed into a transit van that my dad and uncles had hired, piled all our gear in then off we all went down to Somerset. When we pulled up near to Glastonbury my mum took over the driving as we neared to the festival entrance and then everyone jumped out leaving mum me and Terry to wait in the queue. We watched as my dad, along with my uncles all ran and climbed over the fence, disappearing into the festival site. Mum carried on driving and soon she had made it inside. We found a suitable place to pitch the tents near to the pyramid stage, so they could get a good view of the bands. Not long after dad joined us, he had made it in unscathed as did my uncles.

Back in them days, getting in Glastonbury without paying is what everyone did. You couldn't even attempt it now; the festival has gone that big, it's a massive event seen worldwide. You have to apply for tickets months in advance with passport pictures as ID, but back then Glastonbury was much different. It was a CND festival later alongside Greenpeace, in the early 80s and up to around 1986 or 1987 the police weren't even allowed into the festival. There was an agreement in place that prevented the police from entering the site, they had to stand outside watching from afar. It was an unbelievable experience to have been there.

We had our faces painted and we could just roam around, enjoying the atmosphere, mainly doing what we wanted without a care. People getting freely stoned and taking other things. The fact no police were on site made it more open, adding to the atmosphere. I don't remember anything about the bands that were on. I have seen since that the Smiths played and I would have loved to have seen them. Maybe I did, who knows? I can't remember. All I remember it was hot all weekend and that is about it.

We returned to Glastonbury a couple of years later in 1986, this time we travelled down in my dad's Ford Cortina A few years later dad got a picture framed of a crowd shot from that year at Glastonbury where you could clearly see our car amongst the vast crowds. We had that picture hanging in the house for years.

Dad always had a thing about being obscure and different with his cars or work vans, He once had a white Cortina and he got one of his friends to recreate the cover of Bob Marley's Uprising album on the front bonnet. It looked brilliant to be fair and it was something that certainly got the neighbours talking.

One time, after the festival had finished, dad decided that on the way home we would take a detour to Stonehenge. We joined the convoys of hippies who were making their way there for the annual mid summer's eve ritual. Me and my brothers found all this amusing, as we sat in the back of the car whilst looking at the rows of police trying to keep everyone in our convoy away from the area. Mum and dad had seen enough so we turned around setting off home and we never did get to visit Stonehenge and that would be the last time that I went to Glastonbury. Mum and dad carried on for a while but it was getting too commercialised and the festival started losing what it stood for so they stopped going.

After dad died, Terry and mum were both at Glastonbury in 2009. They arranged to meet up in front of the pyramid stage to watch one of my dad's favourite artists, Neil Young, headline on the Friday night. It was a fitting moment with them both there together.

We never had chance to go abroad for our summer holidays, we simply couldn't afford it so, like hundreds of other families in the same position, we instead went to holiday camps or camping in Wales. One year we went to Butlins at Barry Island in

South Wales. It was a long journey with a few breaks for refreshments along the way, and a hot week and we enjoyed the time together participating in family events. Me and dad won the donkey derby and were given rosettes that we saved for years. We also went to Butlins at Pwllheli a few years later. Mum and dad always made sure that we had a break and we had some good times.

Sometimes we had some bad experiences, like the time we went camping in Snowdonia. We went with another family who we were friends of mum and dad and decided to set up camp at the bottom of the Snowdonian mountain, which would have been fine except it rained heavily for days and our camp was totally flooded out. Everything was soaking wet through. All our clothes, the sleeping bags the lot. Mum took us to find a launderette in a nearby town, where she tried to dry it all so we could salvage what was left of the holiday. After we had got everything dry, we returned to the camp site where it had stopped raining. No sooner had we finished our tea and settled down for the night, the heavens opened again, it carried on raining all through the night, meaning everything mum had dried was now soaking wet again. It was decided that it was the end of the holiday, everyone had enough. We packed up what we could salvage then returned home.

We would always be going out on day trips. Mum and dad would pack me and my brothers in the car then off we would go spending days out at the seaside or wherever mum and dad fancied. There were days when the weather was nice and I would come home from school to find mum had made up a picnic. We would wait for dad to finish work then we go and find a spot in the hills or we would go to Macclesfield forest, enjoying a few hours in the sun. I look back on these times and I wonder where did it all go wrong for our family. Back then we were really close, we used to spend loads of time together.

I was starting to try to earn a bit of spending money doing odd jobs here and there. Nothing fancy, just stuff like washing people's cars but that didn't last long, I had started looking for something else to do when I spotted an advert in the newsagents looking for a paper boy. I called in and spoke to the manager who gave me a trial delivering the

Manchester Evening News around the estate. The round didn't take that long and I enjoyed it so much that I was given the round on a permanent basis. I was made up with that because everyone was after a permanent round and they were highly sought after, especially in those days because on Friday you had to go round with your little book and collect the week's money that was owed. I then took the money back to Mr Ray who would make sure it tallied up, then you would get your wages.

On collection days you would always get a few tips from the customers and I always made sure that I did a good job because this meant that you would often get a few quid extra. After about a year of delivering that paper, I was offered a morning round as well. One had come free and did I want it? This was a big thing because doing a morning round meant getting up at six o'clock. I said I would speak with my mum and dad first. My parents thought about it and said OK and providing I wasn't late for school I could give it a go. Unfortunately, I was soon in for a shock.

The round was massive and all the customers' morning paper choices were the Guardian or the Telegraph and some days they had the supplements inside as well so it was heavy going. This round took over an hour to complete then it was back home for breakfast before school. I didn't keep it for long and gave it to one of my mates and just kept the evening one.

I was finishing my round one night when I got to the shop and I saw an advert for someone to deliver the free newspaper The Macclesfield Times. I rang them up and they said that I could deliver three hundred and fifty papers to the area around the estate and I would get paid a penny a paper. I thought I would give it a go but a few days later a van pulled up outside our house and as soon as he was unloading the bundles I realised that I had made a big mistake. My dad talked me into doing it so that Saturday morning off I went with two full bags on my shoulders. It took me hours and I had to go back home when my bags was empty to get some more papers, then walk back to where the last paper was posted and then carry on until I had delivered them all. It was torture and all this for £3.60. It didn't help that my mates were all playing football on the school field while I was walking past them delivering my 'penny a paper'. I wasn't happy.

So, when I got back home, I told my dad that I wasn't doing it anymore and that didn't go down well. I was told that I was going to give it a go because I had said I would do it so I had to carry on. I spent the next month arguing with my dad about it, dreading the time when the van would pull up. One time I refused to deliver them and dad was going mad at me. I was crying saying I wasn't doing it with my dad screaming that I was and my mum in the middle trying to sort this out. Dad shouted that he had had enough of it and started loading the papers up in the car. He then told me to get in and drove me round to the first house on the route. I didn't have a lot of choice so reluctantly I started delivering the papers, whilst he followed me in the car making sure I delivered them all. When my bag was empty, he was there to load me up again. We stayed out until I had completed the round and returned home in silence.

I thought that would have been the end of it and he would let me jack the round in but no, the following month the same ritual continued. More arguments, me sulking until the van pulled up again and the papers were unloaded into the kitchen. This time I was delivering those papers on my own and that was the end of the matter.

The following morning dad had gone to work, so I started delivering the newspapers and it was raining/ I was totally fed up with the task so I delivered the first bag and started the next one when I had a brainwave. On Delemere Drive there are some garages that back onto the canal so I decided to dump the bag of newspapers in there and returned home for another bag which went the same way. Soon I had dumped nearly all of the papers but decided to post the last few thinking I was clever. Unfortunately for me I didn't get to bask in glory for long.

As I made my way home thinking I wouldn't get rumbled, I turned the corner of Dunster Road and my heart sank. Dad had just pulled up from work. He had finished early. There was no way I had delivered the newspapers that quick. As I walked in my dad asked me where the papers were? I replied that I had delivered them all, Dad then looked at me and asked me again, I gave the same response but this time I was going red in the face giving the game away and dad told me to get in the car and said that he was going to drive around to the houses, knock on a few random doors to see if they had received their newspapers. Well that was game over, I had to come clean about my little scam. My dad went mad and made me go and get them, but they were ruined in the rain, He was so mad that he made me give up my evening round as punishment. I never delivered another newspaper again. I could see what dad was trying to do, installing in me his work ethic, teaching me that if you want money you need to go and earn it. He was right but back then I would never have seen that.

You would have thought that I would have learnt a valuable lesson here, but sadly for me and my family, this would not be the first time or last time that I would let my parents and brothers down.

☐ Chapter 5 – Early Morning Run Ins

My relationship with my family was becoming strained and difficult. I was a typical teenager who thought he knew everything and no one was telling me what to do. I would not listen to what mum and dad were saying to me and I was in denial thinking to myself 'what do they know?' They could see a change in me, and they did not like what they were seeing. I was around 15 or 16 years old coming into my final year at school and able to get good GCSEs and plan my future. This should have been my priority but sadly it was not.

I went into the last year of my schooling with the attitude that I would just see it out, have a laugh then leave into the big wide world with what I had. I wasn't thick, I had a brain and I had the ability to get some good grades in a couple of subjects at least but I didn't. I focused my energy everywhere but where it should have been.

The rows that I had with my parents over this were becoming daily. The more that my mum and dad would go on about my attitude, especially with my lack of effort at school, the worse I got. I became stubborn and I had the mind set of what do they know? I knew what was best for me, revising at night for a History or Geography exam wasn't on my list of priorities. I was changing into a different person and it was causing problems within my family.

I was still playing a lot of football with the school team and also Bollington Juniors on a Saturday afternoon. That year the school team reached the quarter final of the English Schools cup but we got beaten in a close game by a school from Blackpool.

After every game Adam Bostock who was in my year at school and played for both teams, started doing write-ups of the games we played with Bollington Juniors. They started appearing in the Macclesfield Express and I was the leading goal scorer, banging them in for fun, so most weeks I would get a mention in the paper. On a Thursday the Macc Express would be delivered to the shop about half six-ish. After tea I would get the paper money and run around to the shop and wait for it to be delivered. I would then run back home to see what the write up would be and after everyone had read it, I would then cut it out and put it in my collection. I headlined most weeks, scoring four, five, six even seven goals some games and I finished the season the leading goal scorer with about forty.

Bollington Juniors held an awards evening at Manchester City F.C social club and we went down on a coach with our parents. It was a great night with all the lads wearing shirt and ties, looking our best. I won the leading goal scorer award and came runner up for Club Player of the Year, mainly because I voted for the winner. He deserved to win the award because he was excellent that season.

The following season we played in the open aged league, and changed the name to Bollington United because we were 16 now and not a junior club anymore. The club is still going strong to this day and opened a new clubhouse not long ago. They still play on the same pitches that we played on thirty years ago.

My GCSE exams were fast approaching and my parents were trying to get me to revise and knuckle down for the final few months that I had left at school, I did the bare minimum for revision. I just wanted the exams to be over so I could be out of there. I left school in the summer of 1989 with no GCSEs, no qualifications, nothing. I wasn't bothered because my attitude was "Don't worry I'll be fine; I don't need any qualifications" much to my parents' dismay.

I remember taking one exam, I think it was Geography and I walked into the exam hall sat at the assigned desk that we were given to take the test and at the designated time when we were told to put our names on top of the exam paper and begin the exam. I put my name on top of the paper as requested and then put the pen down and sat there for the duration with my arms folded, looking at the clock thinking I was being clever. As you can imagine that went down well, the teacher went mad at me, the school informed my parents who went mad at me but my defence was I wasn't going to need a Geography GCSE, so why bother taking the exam. That fell on deaf ears and I was made to take the exam again on my own. The damage was done though and it made no difference because I failed the subject as expected. My schooling was over and it was time to head into the real world.

The day after I left school, I went to France with my uncle Frank. We were going to meet Uncle Tony, who was already there and the plan was that we would help him in renovating the barn that he had bought. We caught the ferry to St Malo where Tony met us and stopped at some services. I had a walk around the shops and started reading a magazine. Tony shouted me that we were going so I walked out. The next thing I know is I was pinned up against the wall by a security guard who was shouting at me in French. I realised then I still had the magazine in my hand and he must of thought that I was stealing it. After some explaining we were finally allowed on our way and we spent a week helping Tony with his barn.

I had now left school so it was time to start thinking about what I was going to do with my life. I was happy to spend all-day lying-in bed, doing nothing much except heading out to see my mates. My dad certainly wouldn't have that for long. He knew someone who had a company called DOR Construction and they took me on under the YTS scheme as an apprentice bricklayer. My wages were £29.50 a week for the first year and then it was supposed to go up in the second. I didn't last long and it was a couple of months at the most before I had enough and left the scheme.

I then joined Royal mail as a postal cadet with my old school mate Peter. A postal cadet is basically an apprentice postman. We would become postmen when we turned 18. I enjoyed working on the post because it was a good job in those days but nothing like it is now with cutbacks ruining the mail industry. The only problem I had was getting up at five o'clock in the morning to start my shift at 6.00am. I used to set my alarm for 5.00am, but I always used to sleep through it or I would put it on snooze and I would sleep through this as well. This would result in my dad coming into my bedroom, trying to get me up for work and an argument would break out meaning everyone would be awake due to me oversleeping.

I would sometimes leave a note on my alarm clock saying something like "when alarm goes off get up and make dad a brew and he will drop me off at work" and things like that. Unfortunately, dad would inevitably come charging into my room shouting at me to get up, sometimes tipping the mattress over and leaving me on the floor. A full-scale row would break out yet again, all this would be before half five in the morning.

My mail route used to take me around the Upton Priory estate, and I was getting back to the sorting office quickly where I would meet up with the other posties who had finished their rounds and join them playing pool in the basement of the sorting office. Postmen used to start early and finish early, usually around 12.30pm, meaning we had the afternoons free. When I first started, I would go straight home getting back in bed for a couple of hours sleep but the other posties used to go to the Royal Oak near to the sorting office for a few afternoon pints. Soon I would start joining them, finishing up at teatime before heading home to eat my tea then head straight to bed.

Things soon started going wrong which was not surprising as my attitude was causing more problems at home. I was becoming out of control and it was affecting everyone. If it weren't me not getting up, it was my attitude towards everything because I wouldn't listen to anyone. I thought I was a man when in fact I was a boy. I was 17, earning a few quid, paying a bit to my mum for my keep and thinking that I could now do what I wanted. I was immature, thinking that I had made it. All I made was resentment from my family who were getting sick of me and my attitude. I couldn't see the effect that my behaviour was having on my brothers. My parents were having trouble with Danny because he wouldn't settle at school. He was playing up which added to my mum's troubles, yet I wasn't bothered because everything had to be about me. The reality is I loved my family, but I was in my own world, a selfish immature place that would lead me to a quite different world, sooner than I would imagine.

I was progressing through the royal mail doing different jobs, thinking that I would make a career as a postman, when things started unravelling for me. For the past few years, I had been best mates with a lad called Nick who lived on the green at the bottom of our road. We became close, spending a lot of time together and playing football and cricket, we were inseparable. When I left school and found a job, I started spending less and less time with Nick. We didn't fall out or anything like that, we just started going in different directions. When I say we, what I am trying to say is that I started going in a different direction.

On the estate there is a row of shops with flats above them. When I went to the shops with Nick or by myself, I would have to walk through the groups that were there. I knew most of them so I was alright and I used to stop and say hello to who was there. One day I was walking over when I bumped into Peter Skerritt.

I went to school with Skez all through Infants and Juniors but I went to Tytherington and he went to Macc High, so we had gone our separate ways. I used to see him around but I didn't knock about with him. Skez was with Rob Hewitt who was a year older than me. I knew who Rob was, but I didn't know him well at all but we got talking and I stayed around the shops with them that evening. We weren't doing anything apart from sitting on the benches and it was pretty boring to be honest. At the same time, I was intrigued in the whole scene especially with Rob so I started spending most of my time with the two of them, mostly sat around the shops. Not doing much but enough to be seen by others. As you can imagine this wasn't going down well at home.

Dad was working on the new daily mirror plant that was being built near Oldham, doing long hours which meant that he wasn't around as much, but when I did see him, more often than not we would end up arguing over my attitude.

I was going out to work then, when I finished my shift, I would come home, get changed then go and stand outside the shops with Skez and Rob until it was late. I would then walk home thinking I was being clever, staying out late knowing I had to get up at five in the morning to start my shift on the post. Inevitably I would sleep through my alarm, which would result in dad coming into my room to turn the alarm off before it woke the house up. He would then have to wake me up for work and within five minutes we would be rowing because dad wouldn't give me a lift, so I was late yet again.

It was my own fault that I was constantly late for work but I would never dream of doing what any normal person would do which would be have an early night and get up when the alarm went off. Instead I blamed my dad for starting the rows in the morning. I wouldn't listen to what my parents were saying to me because in my eyes all they were trying to do was stop me from going out and enjoying myself. They were the ones in the wrong, they were the ones who were making my life hard. Why couldn't they leave me alone? My attitude and behaviour in the home were becoming more and more strained and something had to give. My family was becoming sick and it was decided that it would be best if I went to stay at Nana Costello's for a couple of weeks to give everyone a break.

Nana had moved into a two-bedroom bungalow so there was a spare room available for me to stay in and hopefully things would settle down and I could return home. This was the first time that I was asked to move out, so it came as a bit of a shock. Unfortunately, it wouldn't be the last but at the time I was upset by what had gone on. I resolved to sorting myself out and soon I was back home treading an exceptionally fine line that would quickly give way.

Chapter 6 – A Storm is Brewing

Social drinking, binge drinking, call it what you want, but drinking alcohol changed me. It was like a switch inside me went off every time I drank. It changed me into a different person, a horrible person. I became violent and aggressive and I had no filter once I was drunk. It started becoming a problem almost straight away, with trouble on every front and I can put most of it down to booze.

From the age of 15 my attitude was causing problems at home and now that I had left school and was working, my attitude had gotten a lot worse. The fact that I was drinking meant more problems for my family and as usual it was everyone else with the issues. I was just having a good time.

The first time that I got served in a pub was when I was still at school. A group of us decided to save our dinner money and on the Friday night we would meet up and go for a pint. The plan was to meet at the shops and get the bus to Bollington. Where the bus terminates there was a pub facing it called the Turner's Arms. The Friday night came and I made my way to the meeting point to be met by only two of my school mates. I asked where the rest of the lads were but it appeared, they had got cold feet, Undeterred we caught the bus. I was nervous but at the same time putting on a brave face as we had been told that this pub did underage drinking so we should be fine. The bus pulled into the terminus, we climbed off and slowly headed away. The idea was to find a table in the corner, sit there, then one of us would go to the bar and order the drinks. We walked in through the doors and headed straight for the table furthest away from the bar. It was so obvious that we were underage just by our actions. We sat down then immediately started arguing about who was going up to order the drinks. All the bravado had gone until Stephen said he would go.

It felt like hours before he returned triumphantly, with three pints of best bitter and a packet of fags from the cigarette machine. I asked him who were the fags for seeing none of us smoked. He said if we smoked, we would look older, so Stephen and Andrew took out a cigarette and both sparked up, bearing in mind they had never smoked in their lives. I sat back laughing at them both trying to smoke, it was comical. It took us ages drinking the pint of bitter because no one liked the taste. It was disgusting and I asked Stephen why he didn't get pints of lager. He said he got flustered and the man who got served before him ordered bitter so he just ordered the same. We finally finished our pints and walked out.

Soon I progressed to going round mates' houses drinking old English cider that we would get from an off-licence that one of us could get served in. We would club together and get a bottle of cider to share. We used to head to some garages to drink it and I remember drinking half and that was me gone, my head was spinning, and I felt sick. Luckily, I was staying at my mate's house so we managed to make our way there to sleep it off. When I was still at school there wasn't much drinking to be had, and it was only when I left school that is when I started drinking more. I was finishing work then heading to the pub with a few lads from work. This was becoming daily and it wasn't just a couple of pints then home, it was becoming four or five.

My attitude was becoming intolerable and now I was coming home with an afternoon's drinking under my belt. Things were going downhill fast. My parents would try and talk to me, to no avail. I refused to listen and I didn't care what they had to say. I was in control of my life and I'd be dammed if I was going to listen to mum and dad. Terry and Danny were still at school but that meant little to me. I carried on doing what I wanted, not thinking or acknowledging the effect it had on them and their schooling. The rows that this caused, especially with my dad, should have made me see sense, I should have listened to him. He could see that I was hanging around with the wrong people, he could see that they were no good for me and it upset him because he wanted more for me, so what did I do? I went straight to the shops with Skez and Rob drinking lager thinking I was something special. We would just stand there drinking, it was pathetic really, but it made me feel important, it made me feel part of something although what I do not know. All that I was doing was driving a wedge between me and my family. I was starting to get a reputation and sadly that meant more to me than my family. I stopped going home as much, I was more interested in being with my mates and building this fantasy world. My job started suffering because I was becoming unreliable and missing shifts due to being hungover. Luckily, I had a good boss who looked out for me so I got a few bollockings and nothing more but that wouldn't last long before the big bosses noticed my attitude and I was pulled in and given a warning.

My drinking was becoming daily now. Skez was drinking a bottle of Cinzano washed down with a can of Special Brew. Rob was drinking cans of it. I was drinking Holsten Pills or other strong lager. We would drink our beers sat on the benches outside the shops. Night after night it would be the same pattern. The difference is we started becoming more and more of a problem. I had been fortunate that I wasn't getting into serious trouble. My attitude wasn't just confined to my parents' house, it was following me into my workplace and onto the estate.

My first brush with the police was when I was about 13. I was in town with a couple of mates, when we went into Halfords, in Macclesfield town centre and were looking at BMX stickers to put on our bikes. I saw one lad put some stickers in his pocket. he then looked at me and walked out of the door without paying. My stomach was in knots, I was hot and sweety and why I don't know. I grabbed some too, put them in my coat pocket and walked out of the shop. I didn't get far though as I was collard by the security guard, who marched me into the back room. The police were called and I was taken home to the almightiest bollocking I had ever received.

Now with me running amok around the estate with my mates, drinking and getting up to all sorts, it was only be a matter of time before I would get into trouble again. One Friday night I went out with a couple of work mates from the post office. We had a few pints before heading out and I was having a good time until I went into the toilet and I was punched in the head for no reason. This caught me off guard, it was totally out of the blue and it was over quicker than it started but I was fuming. I found out later that it was mistaken identity and wasn't meant for me. The lad did apologise a long time later. However, I came out of the toilet fuming and carried on drinking to the point where I was really drunk, raging and getting aggressive until I was asked to leave by the bouncers.

I was outside the pub getting myself worked up. Now that I had been thrown out my head had gone. I went over to where Margin Music is and punched my fist straight through the window breaking it in a rage. The bouncers of the pub shouted at me so I ran off home. I arrived still fuming and my dad was still up but I went straight to bed and the next thing I know is two police officers knocked on the door. My dad let them into the kitchen where they asked me if I had broken the window. I said yes and started apologising. I was drunk and I was shitting myself because I had brought the police to my parents' house, I was mortified and dad asked what had happened but I couldn't string a sentence together because I was blind drunk and I was panicking thinking that I was going to be arrested. My dad spoke to the police who explained that it was just one small windowpane that had been broken, so dad offered to pay for it to put an end to the matter. The police said they would speak to the shop owner to see if he wanted to press charges. When the police went, I burst into tears. I was a blubbering mess, I kept apologising, promising that I wouldn't do it again. Dad told me to go to bed to get some sleep and in the morning, we would talk about it.

The following morning, I was feeling sorry for myself, I was hungover and worried sick about what was going to happen. For once I was quiet, listening to my mum and dad telling me this had to stop and that things were getting out of hand. The last thing I wanted was a criminal record. I was 16 nearly 17 and I had only left school about six months ago so things were certainly getting out of hand.

That afternoon the police returned and said I was lucky. The shopkeeper was happy that I paid for the damage, meaning that would be the end of the matter. I was given a talking to by the officers, telling me what would happen next time if I did it again but I assured them that I had learnt my lesson.

Dad paid for the window and I paid him back the following week, grateful that it was the end of the mater. You would have thought that this would have brought me back in line and I would have changed my ways, putting my family first. Toeing the line, knuckling down at home and at work. You would be wrong though. I stayed in for a couple of days but soon I was back out with my mates drinking outside the shops like nothing had gone on. Rob had been in trouble with the police too. He was on bail for a couple of offences, and with my close call with the police it seemed that me and him were bonding more and more. I was looking up to him like he was some sort of leader, he seemed dangerous because he wasn't bothered about going to court, well at least he didn't show it. Rob was older than me and Skez too so that had an effect on me.

At the end of January 1990, I had turned 17. I was getting into more and more trouble around the estate, nothing that would involve the police yet but only through luck. It was like a self-destruct button had been triggered. I was going totally off the rails heading for a massive fall. I had left school six months ago with no qualifications and started a YTS job but that wasn't for me, so I was extremely fortunate to find a job on the post working for the Royal Mail. This should have been the start of my working life, but within five months I would throw all that away, along with my freedom.

I was really arrogant thinking that I was more important than my family. It didn't matter to me what they were going through. It didn't matter as long as Marc Costello was alright doing what he wanted. Absolutely selfish and horrible but unfortunately this was just the start.

Rob, Skez and me started knocking around a house on the estate that two sisters lived at, going round a couple of nights a week, drinking and having a laugh. This soon turned into going around every night and most of the time staying there instead of going home. Before long we had taken the house over and everyone was coming and going as they pleased. Once we were walking from the shops towards the girls' house, when I noticed there was a lad walking towards us, I didn't know him but Rob did and the next thing I know is that Rob had punched him in the head, and in the face. He fell to floor where Skez joined in and the next thing I know is the lad gets up and runs off. I turned to Rob asking him what all that was about to which he laughed and said that he never liked the guy. I couldn't believe it had happened and it was over in less than a minute and all for nothing. We carried on and soon we were round the girls' house drinking and laughing about it.

A few days later we heard that the police were looking for Rob over the assault and Rob was shitting it because he was already on bail for other things and he said he would be going to jail if he got done. We talked about what we were going to do when Rob asked if I would say it was me who assaulted the guy because I hadn't been in trouble with the police and it would be a slap on the wrist, nothing more. Rob was pleading with me saying he was going to jail if he got done. I should have walked away, telling him to get fucked but instead I agreed, thinking that it was a good idea. Was it peer pressure? I don't think so. I had misplaced loyalties; I would rather throw my future away by getting a criminal record for a crime I took no part in.

Life spiraled out of control heading one way, down into the depths of despair, the self-destruct button had been pressed. This one event set the tone for the life that I was about to enter, a life that I am still trying to forget. I can't really blame Rob; it was my decision. Life is about choices and I made the wrong one. I didn't think about how this would affect me and my future. I was working for the Royal Mail and I knew that if I got a criminal record then I would lose my job but the thought of that never entered my head.

I never once gave any thought to what my parents and brothers would think. I was so selfish that I couldn't care less what anyone thought. My mate needed help and I was going to help him come what may. Rob should have been a man, accepted what he had done and faced the music, no one forced me to take this charge even though it wouldn't end well for me.

The day after the police arrested me, Skez and Rob on suspicion of assault. We were taken to Macclesfield police station, processed and then placed in separate cells. This was the first time that I had been arrested and I was putting on a brave front, acting like I wasn't bothered. I refused to have a solicitor and went to get interviewed.

The policeman asked me all sorts of questions in relation to what had happened on the night in question. I told him that I had assaulted the guy and he asked me why. I didn't know why Rob had punched him, so I just said for no reason, which was my big mistake because that would go against me when I went to court. The interview was concluded and I was placed back in my cell.

A short while later me and Skez were in front of the sergeant who informed us that we were both being charged with section 47 Assault and bailed to appear before the magistrates in a few weeks. I was 17, on bail for assault and as you can imagine my parents were furious with me, especially when I told them that it was Rob and Skez that had done it and I had nothing to do with it. My dad was all for going out to find Rob until I said I would never speak to him again. It was pathetic, defending him over my parents, putting my mates before my family yet again.

My mum and dad were truly despairing with me and my behaviour but I didn't care. I just thought they were having a go at me, the only thing I was bothered about was my mates. I was now getting a name for myself, building a reputation and people were talking about me and not in a good way. I was loving this, thinking I was some big man, trouble was coming thick and fast and it wasn't long before I was arrested again.

Chapter 7 – Four Cans and a Bottle of Cider

Drinking was becoming a problem for me. It was starting to change me and my attitude was becoming nasty towards people. I was walking around thinking I was something special, especially when I had a can in my hand. You would have thought with me being on bail for assault, that would have made me think about my actions, but you would be wrong.

We were spending most of our time around the girls' house drinking strong lager and cider when one night a lad who was seeing one of the girls stormed off after a row with her. He had left his car parked outside the house and the girl was fuming so I decided with Skez to get a white spray can and spray names all over his car. We were both drunk, thinking this was a great laugh and we sprayed the car until it wasn't black anymore, then went back in the house to carry on drinking and laughing at our masterpiece.

We fell asleep only to be woken up the following morning, by the lad banging on the door wanting to know what on earth had happened. I said we had done it for a laugh but we had ruined his car and in the cold light of day you could see there wasn't anything funny about it.

Not long after, the police turned up with the lad. He told them what had gone on and said it was me and Skez and he wasn't happy. The police asked us if we had done it so I said yes, we had. There was no point in lying. What had started as a bit of fun had escalated into vandalism. We were arrested and taken to Macclesfield police station, where we were both charged with criminal damage and bailed to appear at the magistrates at the same time as the assault charge.

I was still working at the Royal Mail at this time but only because I haven't said anything to the bosses about my impending court case. I thought if I didn't say anything then they might not find out, that's how naïve I was at the time. Nothing to do with the fact it was a sackable offence to get into any trouble with the police. I was hanging on to the job and my home life by a very thin piece of rope, that was fraying all the time.

A few weeks later on a Saturday night, Rob was going to meet a girl he was seeing from the western estate in Macclesfield. Me and Skez tagged along and bought a load of booze to see us through the evening. The plan was for us to have a few drinks, then call round the girls' house to have a bit of a party. We were having a laugh getting drunk and the time was getting on and Rob was late for meeting his girlfriend so we finished up and headed off. We still had a few cans left but when we arrived the girls weren't happy because we were off our heads. We started getting rowdy, singing and shouting, until the girls had enough of us and told us to leave. I refused, saying we weren't going anywhere because we hadn't done anything. The girl whose house it was said we either left or she would phone the police. I picked up a can of lager up ready to crack it open, with the girl was telling me to put it down and get out. I threw it straight through the back-door window, the glass shattering everywhere.

The girls were screaming for us to get out, it was bedlam, I just staggered off thinking fuck it.

I didn't get very far until I heard the sirens. Two police cars came flying up the road. One went past me, the other one pulled up next to where I was stood. Two policemen jumped out and grabbed hold of me and I heard a police officer say over the radio that it was me that had damaged the window. So, I got arrested for criminal damage. I was handcuffed, searched, then taken to the police station where I was kept overnight to face another charge on my growing list.

I woke up in the cell the following morning, not remembering that much about what had gone on the night before and trying to piece together what I had done. A police officer came to interview me and that's when the facts emerged. Another stupid drunken moment, for no reason apart from the fact I couldn't handle my drink. I was charged with criminal damage again and bailed. I walked out of the police station, feeling nothing but pissed off. I was hungover, and I was going to have to face my parents.

They were astounded by my actions, and just couldn't understand what I was doing. They tried to talk to me, to tell me that I couldn't carry on the way I was, that the effect that my actions were having on everyone in the family, tearing the house apart. My response was to row with them and accuse them of being killjoys. Who did they think they were trying to stop me from going out and having fun?! In my selfish mind, going out drinking with my mates, getting up to all sorts of shit, causing problems everywhere I went was my idea of a good time. I thought I knew everything when in fact I knew nothing.

Rob was having trouble at his house as well, he was always falling out with his dad over the shit he was getting into, so we both decided that we were going to leave home and find somewhere to live where we could do as we pleased. I went to see my uncle Frank and he said that we could move into his spare bedroom. I went home and proudly announced that I was moving out. Dad wasn't pleased at all because Frank had his own problems and me and Rob adding to them wouldn't end well but I was adamant that I was going. I packed a bag and off me and Rob went to stay at Frank's flat.

I was excited to live there as I was still working on the post but my time there would come to an end very soon. I still hadn't mentioned my arrests, seeing as I hadn't actually been convicted of anything yet. I was missing days and becoming very unreliable but soon that would become irrelevant. The slope that I was on was becoming very slippery.

Living with Frank became a routine of drinking every day after work (if I made it in to work) and at weekends we would drink until we didn't know what we were doing. Frank was doing his own thing with his friends in the living room so we were left to do what we wanted.

One Saturday in 1990 things got a lot worse for me. I have no defence, no excuse, it was cowardly and I still regret it now. I got up that morning to find Rob and Frank had started drinking cider that we had left over from the night before; I had a glass then we decided to go and get some more from the off-licence. Skez had joined us so we all went off.

We were soon back with loads of cider, with Guns 'n' Roses blasting on the stereo. I was drinking my can of cider, singing along and having a good time. Frank was showing off, drinking pints of cider in one, necking them down. He poured another one took a mouthful and threw up all over the living room, Skez, Rob and me were pissing ourselves at Frank who was coughing his guts up and were extremely drunk at this point. I was absolutely off my head and had drunk at least six litres of cider when we decided to walk up to Hurdsfield. Why I don't really know, it must have seemed a good idea at the time.

Things were a bit blurry at this point and apparently, we were in the pub trying to play pool and drinking more cider. We were getting out of order, much to the annoyance of the landlord who asked us to leave. I walked outside the pub and came across an old man who was walking to his car carrying a small bike, which I found out after was a present for his young daughter whose birthday it was that day. I shouted "Oi! What are you looking at?" as I staggered towards him and punched him in the head. Why I don't know, as I had never seen him before in my life. As I hit him, I fell over and he grabbed me, shouting to his wife to call the police, with her helping him to pin me down. The fact that I was out of my head on cheap cider meant I couldn't move.

A couple of minutes later the sirens could be heard. The police arrested me for assault and took me to the police station where I collapsed into a drunken stupor until the morning. I woke up, realising that I was in the cells and my heart sank. I felt sick, my mouth was dry and my head was spinning with the thought that I had fucked up again. This time it was different. I had no clue what I had actually done. Was I on my own? Were Skez and Rob in here as well. I couldn't think straight. I remembered being at Frank's flat then that was about it. A policeman came into my cell to take me to the custody desk where a sergeant was stood behind the counter. He commented that now I was sober we could start again because apparently when I was arrested, I was in no fit state to speak never mind do much else and I had been placed in the drunk cell to sleep it off.

The sergeant told me that I was being held on suspicion of causing GBH and would I like a solicitor to represent me. My mind was spinning. GBH, me! Who on? Jesus, what had happened?! I was in the shit and I could not remember anything about it. I told the sergeant that I didn't want one although at that point I should have. I had been arrested four times within a couple of months.

I was placed back in my cell with a cup of tea and waited to be interviewed. I was worried because I had never been in this position before and sat there feeling sorry for myself, hungover and sick to my stomach about what I had done.

Later I got taken to the interview room where I was told in detail what had gone on the day before. It was spelt out to me that I had assaulted this man for no reason at all. I had spoilt his daughter's birthday party and I was an absolute disgrace to society. I sunk in my chair feeling mortified. I hadn't been brought up like this, so how could this have happened? The incident took place a few yards from where I had spent many a good time at my nana Naden's house. I had never felt so bad in my life as I did at this point. I couldn't justify any of what the police were saying to me and admitted to everything. There was no point in defending what I had done I just wanted to get out of there.

I was charged with causing GBH, with that added to my other charges meant I was lucky to get bail as the sergeant warned me that if I was arrested before I went to court then I wouldn't be getting it again.

I made my way back to Frank's. When I walked in and found Rob and Skez sat drinking with Frank in the living room, I was feeling pretty sorry for myself and worried about the mess my life was in. I was passed a can and as soon as the first mouthful had hit the back of my throat all my fears went. Soon I was laughing about what had happened. It was business as usual but this time Rob and Skez were bigging me up saying I was off my head; I took it as a massive complement. I felt that I had been accepted, and in our gang, I was one of the main men.

A couple of days later I was woken by someone knocking on Frank's door. I opened it to find the main boss from Macclesfield post office standing there. He introduced himself and said we needed to talk about my position with the Royal Mail and handed me a letter inviting me into a meeting to discuss it. I told him that there wasn't much point because I had got myself into trouble with the police and you couldn't work as a postman with a criminal record. He told me not to be hasty and to attend the meeting which would be held the following week.

I took the easy way out and did not attend which resulted in me getting another visit from the manager, this time with a letter telling me that I had been sacked. I wasn't bothered. It just meant that I did not have to get up early anymore which meant I could stay up doing what I pleased. Drinking was becoming the norm especially with me and Rob living together at Frank's. We had no rules and could come and go as we pleased but unfortunately this ended abruptly.

Rob, Skez and me were sat around Frank's drinking one Saturday afternoon. We were running low on alcohol so Rob said he was going to the off license. A short while later he returned with a bag full of cider and another lad in tow called Grego. He was older than us and lived a couple of floors down from Frank. I personally didn't know him but I had heard of him because he was part of a group who called themselves the Moss Rats. He was into drugs which we weren't so our paths had never crossed.

We carried on drinking and soon Frank came back and when he saw Grego sat in his living room he wanted to know what was going on, because Frank knew who he was and what he was like. We just said he was having a drink with us and would be going soon, Frank said he was going out for the night and told me to make sure we locked the door. We carried on drinking until early evening when we decided to go up town and me, Rob and Skez left, leaving Grego as we headed into town.

I returned to Frank's later that evening to find the flat in darkness. I walked into the living room where I was grabbed by someone and thrown on the settee. The light was switched on and Frank was on top of me holding a hammer, demanding to know where his stereo was. He was screaming at me and waving the hammer about threatening to smash my head in if I didn't tell where it was. I didn't know where his stereo was as I had been in town. My dad turned up and grabbed Frank off me. I looked at where the stereo should have been and it was missing. We had been robbed and Frank was sure I was responsible. I kept saying it had nothing to do with me but the more I said that the irater Frank was getting I couldn't reason with him at all. My dad asked me what had gone on I told him that we had left the flat and headed into town. Frank asked if Grego with me and I said no, he had walked off the other way.

Frank said when he returned home the door was open, I had forgotten to lock the door so someone had walked in knowing everyone was out and nicked the stereo, the only person likely was Grego so he was responsible. Frank went off with the hammer down to Grego's flat but luckily for him he wasn't in. Frank would have killed him that night if he had got hold of him. I was told to get out of the flat. I had nowhere to go so dad grabbed my stuff and took me home.

I was thankful that I could return home but my parents made it clear that things would have to change. I needed to sort my life out and I wouldn't be allowed to continue the way I was going, certainly not under their roof. We spoke about my impending court cases and they didn't judge me but they certainly weren't happy about what had gone on. They said we needed to get a good solicitor to represent me at the hearing.

Mum contacted a solicitor that had been recommended to us and made an appointment. Next day, I told him everything that I was charged with and he applied to get all the paperwork sent over as well as to have all the charges heard at the same time.

I was due in court at the end of April, so we didn't have long to sort my defences out, not that I had one anyway. I appeared at court and pleaded guilty to all four charges and the magistrate adjourned the case for four weeks for pre-sentencing reports. These were to be conducted by the probation service and I was given a time and a date to attend the office where the reports would take place.

My solicitor advised me to find employment as it would look better for me when I went back in front of the bench. I was lucky because I found work straight away at Fairclough's as a chain lad for the engineers. I would hold their sticks whilst they took readings from them on various locations, then we would head back to the offices where they would write all the information up and work out the dimensions whilst I sat there waiting for my next task.

My solicitor had recommended that I should be placed on probation for a year with a compensation order or a fine. There was no mention of anything like prison.

I attended the office for probation who asked me a series of questions about my background, my family life, school, sport things like that, trying to build a background as to what had led me to go off the rails and start offending. I was asked why I committed these offences, so I told them honestly that I had been drinking and I didn't know what I was doing, including the first assault and that I hadn't done it but was covering for Rob. It was soon made obvious that at 17 I was developing a problem with alcohol and I couldn't handle it. I had only been drinking for about six months and the fact was it didn't take me long to get pissed but I would still continue drinking until I didn't know what the fuck I was doing.

The probation officers completed their reports on me, along with what my solicitor was recommending and it was agreed by everyone that they would recommend twelve months' probation with a condition on attending a drink awareness course and a compensation order. I was upbeat, thinking that I could put all this behind me and move on with my life. Things were a lot better at home because I was working. I was still knocking about with Skez and Rob but I had cut down on my drinking. The seriousness of my actions was coming home to roost, I was just focusing on keeping my nose clean getting myself ready for the sentencing hearing in May.

☐ Chapter 8 – A Short, Sharp Shock

As I look back on this day, I take a moment and wonder if the day had ended with a different outcome, what would have become of my life?

Would I have gone down the same route that I did? I am writing this down exactly 30 years ago to the day of my sentencing hearing in the magistrates court and I think of what brought me to this point. Why did I take the blame for what Rob did? Would he have done the same for me? I doubt it very much but who knows, I never asked him. I had been out of school for about ten months and yet here I was standing in the dock of Macclesfield Magistrates Court awaiting sentencing for my actions. It seems unbelievable really when you look at the time scale. I should have been starting out in the big wide world choosing a career that would have embarked me into adulthood yet ten short months had passed since I walked out of Tytherington High School with the same hopes and dreams that my fellow classmates shared. Unfortunately, that was where the similarities ended because our paths went in a quite different way. The path that I was heading down was to become a very lonely, bitter and selfish one.

Today it's Sunday 31st May 2020 and the country is coming out of a lockdown due to a pandemic. Covid-19 is a virus that has shut the world down as we know it for the past three months. Thirty years ago, I was about to enter my own lockdown, one that I am still dealing with. My solicitor, along with the probation office had recommended probation with an alcohol awareness course bearing in mind that this was the first time that I had been in front of a court of law in any capacity. I had a clean record up to this point and that should have gone in my favour, along with the positive reports presented to the court. The fact that I had admitted everything to the police and had pleaded guilty at the first opportunity should also have benefited me in the eyes of the court.

If I had been sentenced as the reports had recommended then would I have continued to get myself into trouble? Would I still have walked around thinking I was someone special? A person with a bad attitude that everyone including my family had had enough of. I would have liked to think that, given the chance to work with the probation officers, the answer is no, especially regarding my problems with alcohol which was the cause of my offending behaviour. The reality is everything that I ever got arrested for stemmed from been intoxicated to the point that I wasn't in control of my actions.

The incidents that engulfed my life in the years and decades after were due to the fact that alcohol was involved so if I had been sentenced to probation then this could have been addressed and maybe I would have gone down the straight and narrow route. Thirty years later I trace everything back to this point. The path that I did go down was a dark place. The verdict of the court put me onto a merry-go-round, that spun faster and faster until years later when it slowed down and I could finally climb off, the damage had been done. Relationships would never be the same and things that happened then, even now all these years later I am still coming to terms with. I am in no way blaming the courts, they punished me accordingly, with the powers that they felt my behaviour warranted. That is their right to do. To send out a message to drunken thugs, who came in front of them that such behaviour will not be tolerated in our society.

My actions were down to me trying to be a big guy, a hard man, but the reality is different. I was a thug who fully deserved everything that was coming to him. It should have been the short, sharp shock the magistrate promised, as he sent me to a young offenders' institution for ninety days. The reality is that, with those words, a chain of events was underway and I came back into society with a reputation. The name Cozzy was being mentioned in wider circles and not just on my estate but around the whole of Macclesfield. With that came trouble and I could handle myself and now, with the added tag of having been in prison I was becoming more of a handful. A reputation was something that I craved for at the time. I thrived off it and everything that followed.

Looking back at this now, I can tell you from my own experience that this reputation that I thought was so important to me, means nothing, not a thing. It's something that even now I am struggling to get away from. I can be out with my wife enjoying a quiet night when people will come up and start talking. I will engage in small talk until I walk away and my wife will ask me who I was talking to and I reply that I haven't a clue. They know the name Cozzy but they don't know Marc. I have had people start fights with because of my name. Cozzy is long gone but the reputation is still there, and I have to deal with it just like I had to deal with the magistrates decision not to give me a probation order and the chance to sort myself out but to send me to a young offenders' institute and into a circle of mayhem that I am still coming to terms with.

I can remember everything clearly about that day, even the clothes that I was wearing. I had light blue jeans with a red paisley shirt and a black waistcoat. You may ask why wasn't I wearing a suit, or a shirt and tie. The honest answer is that it didn't occur to me to. I thought I looked smart enough with what I had on, plus I didn't think the situation I was in warranted a suit. I believed I would walk into the court and I would walk out with a sentence of probation. I never thought for one minute that I would lose my freedom.

Skez was up for sentencing as well as he was my co-accused of the assault that Rob did and the criminal damage on the car. He had the same solicitor as me and after a while he came to see us to discuss what would be happening and when we were called into the court, we were still expecting probation.

The waiting area was getting busy as there was a few of our mates from Hurdsfield that had come down to support us. My mum was also there, which I was grateful for and we sat around talking making plans to have a party at the girls' house later that day to celebrate. There was no thought of any other outcome, and when heard our names called, we made our way into the court.

As we entered the dock, the public gallery was filling up with my mum and all our friends and the usher asked the court to rise as the three magistrates entered. We were then asked to confirm our names and addresses and told to be seated. The prosecutor then outlined the charges to the magistrates and to the fact that we had both pleaded guilty. There were pre-sentence reports available to the magistrates with the recommendations laid out inside. He then started going through the charges one by one outlining what we had done and it suddenly seemed real. Before, the bravado and the image of not giving a fuck had shielded me, but now, sat there with Skez, listening to the facts of the offences being laid bare for everyone, the mask was slipping. Reality had hit me hard, but I couldn't show it to anyone especially not to my mates sat in the courtroom.

When the prosecutor came to tell the court about the GBH charge, I felt appalled by what I was hearing. It felt like they were talking about someone else. I couldn't believe that I was the thug that they were portraying me to be. I was ashamed and I felt embarrassed that my mum had to sit there listening to it all. I still feel bad about this and thirty years later it still affects me and it always will.

The magistrates did not look impressed by what they were hearing and who could blame them?

I was hoping that when my solicitor addressed the court, they would see that I wasn't this person that they had portrayed but deep down I knew that the damage had been done and anything my solicitor said would be damage limitation.

I sat there listening as my solicitor started talking about Skez and his part in the offences. At the end he recommended that they read the pre-sentence reports and followed their recommendations, then he started talking about me. He explained that I had come from a loving home with support from my family and I was employed working on building a new road in the town. He added that drink had played a huge part in my actions and that I had started to address this issue. My solicitor then addressed the final charge of GBH on the old man outside the pub and agreed it was a serious charge that was unprovoked and totally unwarranted and needed punishing, but he told the court about the remorse that I had for this crime and how it had affected me and my family. He explained how I was that drunk that I didn't know what I was doing and said how I was totally co-operative with the police and I had admitted everything and was really remorseful. He reminded the magistrate that I had pleaded guilty at the first opportunity so this should count in my favour. He finished off by repeating what he had said about Skez and following the pre-sentence reports and the recommendations. The magistrates said that they would now retire to their chambers where they would read the reports and consider all the options. All I could do now was wait.

If anyone has ever been in this position you will relate to the feelings experienced. The emotions flowing through your body as you sit in the dock waiting to hear your fate. After what seemed like an eternity the magistrates returned and the chairman of the bench asked me and Skez to stand. He turned to Skez and started to address him saying they had read the pre- sentence reports and his sentence was a compensation order. He was free to leave the dock. Skez shook my hand and wished me luck.

The chairman then looked at me and his face was giving nothing away. He went through the offences, outlining that being drunk was no defence. He went on to say that I had committed a totally unprovoked assault on a man who was doing nothing more than celebrating his daughter's birthday and nothing could justify that behaviour. He called me a drunken thug who would have to be punished and whilst they had considered the pre-sentence reports they felt that the nature of the assault merited a stiffer sentence.

I knew at this point I was fucked and I was not going home tonight. The chairman carried on telling me that they were going to impose a sentence that would act as a short, sharp shock, as he called it, then he announced to the court that my sentence would be ninety days in a young offenders' institution. I was stunned because had I never for one moment thought this would happen. My mum was crying, my friends were in shock no one could believe it. I stood there stunned as the door opened and two police officers walked in. I was placed in handcuffs then taken back through the waiting area and placed in the back of the court in a room where they then removed the cuffs. I was about to ask what would happen next when my solicitor walked in. He told me that he was sorry that the bench had not followed his and the probation guidelines and that the sentence of ninety days meant that I would do half which was roughly six weeks.

I asked him where I was going but he didn't know and neither did the police officer who was there guarding me.

He said I was going to be taken to Macclesfield police station first but after that he was unsure. I asked if I could see my mum which was arranged as she had been outside waiting to see me. She'd stopped crying but was really upset. I felt terrible for putting her through this. I kept saying sorry, which I meant knowing my selfish actions had led me to this point yet knowing I had brought my family along with me and that hurt more. We hugged and then it was time to go. I had the handcuffs put back on and was taken from the room out to where my mates were stood. I said goodbye to them as I was placed into the police car.

We made the short trip across town to the station where I was sat on a bench in the custody suite. My mind was in a blur. I was putting on a brave face but inside I was shitting myself. Where was I going? What would happen to me? I had seen on the news about the recent riots at Strangeways prison in Manchester, that had lasted twenty-five days. It was the longest prison disturbance in British penal history. I knew I was heading to a young offenders' institution and I thought they were the same place as prisons. This is how clued up I was on my situation. With the fact that I was expecting to get probation I had never given prison a second thought until it was too late.

I was informed by the custody sergeant that they were trying to find me a place because, with the situation at Strangeways, there was little space available throughout the system. Prisoners were being kept in police stations across the north west because of the spillover from Strangeways. I was placed in a cell until they knew what was going on but I hadn't been in it long when I was informed that I was going to be taken to a place called Werrington House. I had never heard of it or where on earth it was, so I asked the custody officer who told me that it was in Stoke-on-Trent.

An hour passed when finally, the handcuffs were placed back on as I was put inside the police car to begin the journey to my home for the next six weeks. I didn't know if it would make me or break me but I felt sick with nerves. My mouth was dry, a hundred thoughts going through my mind. The journey didn't take long and my palms were sweaty as we approached the entrance to Werrington House, Young Offenders Institution.

Chapter 9 – 266 Costello, Sir!

As the police car pulled up outside the gates to Werrington House, I suddenly felt so alone. The realisation was setting in. I knew that my life would now be defined by this moment. It wouldn't be the same ever again. A line had been crossed from which there would be no return. The punishment must be seen to fit the crime, that much is true, but I was 17 years old and my future could not and should not have been determined by this.

A prison officer (who I would very soon be told to address as 'sir') approached the car and a file containing paperwork was handed over. He scanned it quickly before shouting to his colleague to open the gates to allow us to enter. We drove into the holding area as the gates were locked behind us. I went to climb out but was told to stay where I was until they called for me.

A few minutes passed and then the officers were told to bring me in to the reception area where I was instructed to empty my pockets and then asked my name address and what my sentence was. I answered all the questions and finished by calling him 'mate', at which point he looked at me and said that he wasn't my mate. I was silent as he told me that officers were to be addressed with 'sir'. My first lesson had been given, He told me to sign for my property and I was then informed that I was now 266 Costello, my prison number.

I was given a towel and told to take off my clothes and hand them to a lad who was in prison clothing. I later found out that this was the reception orderly, a prisoner who is trusted to work in the reception and a privileged position within the prison. I was told to take a bath which was in the adjacent room. I said that I had already had a bath this morning but the officer just stared at me and at that point the orderly said everyone had to have a bath on arrival. I looked at the tub which was thick with grime that looked like it had been there for year. There was about six inches of water inside it and I was expected to climb in with an officer and an orderly standing there watching over me.

I lowered myself into the lukewarm water wondering what the fuck was going on, I had been in the bath a couple of minutes when I was told to get out. The orderly asked me what my waist and jumper size were and I was then handed a pile of prison issue clothes along with two pairs of Y-fronts that were heavily stained by the hundreds that had worn them before me. As I started getting dressed the reception door opened and another lad was led in to go through the same process that I had just gone through. When I was dressed, I was given a bundle of bedding and a pillow and told to sit on a bench and wait for the doctor.

I tried to take it all in the smells, the noise, the atmosphere. I couldn't believe what had happened in the space of a few hours and I knew I needed to get my head around this. There was no point in crying over it, I had to front it out and get on with it because they were not going to let me go. I heard my name being called and walked into the doctor's room where he asked me my name and number.

I thought "number what does he mean?", I said my name was Marc Costello he asked what's my number. I just looked at him with a blank expression. He said the number I had been given in reception, but I didn't know it. The doctor reminded me my number is 266 and I needed to remember it at all times. That was my second lesson.

He then asked me a few questions about my health, then told me to drop my trousers so he could examine me for pubic lice. I also had to 'cough and drop' and then I was told I had a clean bill of health and led back to the bench to wait for my next ordeal.

I was joined on the bench by another newcomer from reception and a few minutes later he was called in to have his balls looked at by the resident doctor. When he came back, we were told to get our clothes and bedding and then led outside.

We went through the gates into a long room with rows of beds down both sides. This was the dormitory where we would be staying. We were shown our beds and lockers and told to make our beds up, then put our stuff away. I hadn't seen any other prisoners yet but found out that they were at work or in education. I unfolded the mattress and couldn't believe what I was seeing. It was filthy! Full of stains and holes. I later learnt this was where some of the previous prisoners had made themselves a gap in the mattress so they could shag it in the middle of the night, and this is what I was meant to sleep on. The Y-fronts were bad enough, never mind the itchy green bedding that I had to use, along with a holey mattress to sleep on in a dormitory with loads of other lads.

I could hear the sound of people talking and it was getting louder. Suddenly, a gate opened at the bottom of the dorm and the other prisoners started returning from work or education. Then I heard "Fuck me Cozzy what are you doing here?" and looked round and saw my mate Lee. I hadn't known Lee was in here but I was glad to see a friendly face. We started talking about old times and Lee was amazed I was in there and asking what I was in for and how long I got. He was out in a couple of weeks as his time was nearly over. He introduced me to a few of the other lads in there who he knocked about with. They seemed alright, with Lee explaining who I was and they welcomed me into to their circle. There was a TV at the end of the dorm and I soon found out that there was a pecking order. New arrivals had the empty beds at the far end. Depending on who you knew or how long you had been in there, the nearer to the TV you got. With me knowing Lee I was moved straight away further up, which was fine by me.

The following morning resembled something like I would imagine being in the army was like. The lights were switched on and the prison officers, or screws, were shouting for everybody to get up. "Hands off cocks and into socks" they shouted, as I lay there not sure what the fuck was going on. I stood at the end of the bed, like the others, wondering what was going to happen next. Then we were told to get our stuff and head to the toilet area, where we washed our faces and brushed our teeth with a bland, hard looking substance, certainly not the Colgate that I was used to.

When we had finished, we were back by our beds ready to make them. Lee came over and told me that we had to make our beds up into a pack. I had never heard of a bed pack before so Lee showed me what I had to do. Then we had to wait to be called for breakfast. This would be repeated every morning and anyone whose bed pack wasn't done to the screws' standards would have it thrown everywhere, so you had to start again, keeping everyone waiting for breakfast. This resulted in fights breaking out because everyone was hungry and wanted feeding so you had to get it right.

With me being a new inmate, I had to do what they called an induction. This was basically to determine if I could work or needed to go to education. There were a lot of youngsters aged between 15 to 17 years old who were held in a separate dormitory and they went straight to education. I was asked a few questions and if I felt suicidal or had any self-harm tendencies which I wasn't and didn't. I was informed of the rules and told that if I wanted someone to visit me then I had to apply for a VO which is a visiting order and this would get sent out to whoever was coming to see me. They would then hand it in at the gate on their arrival. Then I was issued with a letter so I could write to my family.

My mum recently found the letter that I sent to my parents, having kept it in a box all these years. She gave me it recently to look at and reading it again I was ashamed of what I put my family through. I was so selfish and single-minded. All I was concerned about was myself and if I was alright, I had no thoughts about what my family must have been feeling. The shame of their child being labelled a thug and sent to a young offenders' institution; this is something that bothers me to this day. You can see in the letter how selfish I was.

Number 266   Name Costello
HM Y.O.I
Werrington
Stoke on Trent
ST90DX

Dear mum and dad,

well here I am in Werrington Y.O.I, it is alright here I suppose apart from the foods crap and you drink tea with no sugar. We are not in cells, Its one big dormitory where all the seniors sleep. There is another one for all the juniors, people have told me that it is supposed to be the easiest prison in Britain and I can see why, we have got a pool table and a colour television, so I can watch the world cup in here. You remember Lee? Well he is in here and he said he will show me around. I got 90 days, but I should be out in 45 days (6 weeks) if I behave myself. I have sent you a VO so you and Terry can come and visit me, but before that right back to me. Don't forget to find out about my job at Fairclough's and let me know, I might be able to do some work while I am in here, so I will be able buy some things. Hope you have a nice time at Glastonbury and at Knebworth, and don't worry I will be alright, and how is Daniel hope he is alright? Tell Terry to do me a favour and go round to 44 and tell them that I am alright, and to write to me, the address is HM Y.O.I, Werrington, Stoke on Trent thanks Terry I owe you one, cannot wait to be back at home, I am glad that it is only 6 weeks instead of 6 months, well hope to see you soon love you all Marc.

    Ps when you come to visit me will you bring next week's Macclesfield Express so I can read it. Thanks Marc.

I started settling into life at Werrington. There was a lot of bullying going on especially with the first timers like myself who were seen as easy pickings. I was fortunate that I knew Lee and I knocked around with him, and Lee got on with most in the dorm, so that applied to me as well and I didn't get any trouble off anyone.

At the weekend we had to scrub the dorm from top to bottom making it spotless for the governor's inspection that was held on Saturday mornings. We had to have all our kit laid out on our beds followed by shiny shoes and a bed pack done so tightly that you could bounce a coin on it. If you failed the inspection you spent the weekend cleaning everywhere whilst everyone else had association time. This meant you could play football, go to the gym, play pool, and watch television. Visits were also held at weekends. They lasted for an hour and were held in the main hall where the orderlies served up tea and refreshments for the visiting families. I was lucky that I received visits from my family, it must have been difficult for them. They could have turned their backs on me and let me get on with it saying, 'you've made your bed you better lie in it!' I'm thankful that they didn't do that.

Soon it was time for Lee to leave and we said our goodbyes and I moved up the pecking order into his bed space which was nearer to the television. A couple of days later a lad serving a four-month sentence for nicking car stereos called Gary arrived, from Biddulph, not far from Macclesfield. We hit it off from the word go and became good friends and still are to this day. The day Gary got released from Werrington, he moved to Macclesfield where he still lives now.

When Gary arrived, we both started getting into a bit of trouble in the prison, nothing serious just juvenile stuff like cutting the ends of socks, so when the person put their socks on, the end was cut away, we would both crack up laughing. Me and Gary both got a job working maintaining the gardens. One day we were painting some doors when we thought it would be a laugh, if we got some ladders and painted our names on the prison roof, other times we would lie in the gardening carts and go to sleep lying in the sun.

Bullying was rife in Werrington and it was relentless unless you stood up for yourself. I was lucky in the sense that I knew Lee when I arrived and I didn't get any bother of anyone. Then when Gary arrived, we were always together so we didn't get any bullies trying it on with us.

The problem with these young offenders' institutions, is that they are very violent places. You have young teenagers with high levels of testosterone flying around their bodies thinking they are ten men. You learn from the word 'go' that you can never let anyone take a liberty, if you back down over anything then that will be seen as a weakness and will be pounced on. You have kids in these places for petty offences, miles away from their families and when they arrive, they are scared and vulnerable, and cannot look after themselves. The minute they walk in to the dorm they are pounced on, what little personal belongings they had have taken off them, and unless they fight back, they are in for a tough time for the duration of their stay.

I had a run in with a lad from Hull. I forget his name, but for some reason he did not like me. I was getting on with the lads from Stoke and he tried putting me down at every opportunity. When I ignored him, he took to staring at me all the time like he fancied me and it was making me feel uncomfortable. I did not want people in there thinking I was weak.

The time to confront him came when I bumped into him in the toilet, of all places. There was just me and him in there, so I asked him what the fuck was his problem was. He just looked at me and said there was no problem, so I told him to leave it out or settle it now. After a standoff he backed down and walked away. I did not want to fight, but I would have had to. Win or lose you had no choice and he knew that as well as I did. So, we both moved on without losing face.

In the dorm there was a ritual that all the new arrivals had to do, called the bed run. You started at the bottom end of the dorm and had to jump over the first bed then go under the next and so on until you had gone up and over them all. You did this with everyone hitting you with pillowcases stuffed with boots and books, anything that could hurt you. You left with a few bruises but nothing more. I did the bed run on my arrival like everybody did but there was a new lad in the dorm who from the word go was being bullied. He had all his tobacco taken off him, as soon as he walked in, so now he was desperate for a smoke. No one would give him anything. It was sad to see this going on but that was life in there. He got so desperate that he started to smoke tea bags wrapped in strips of the bible that he had torn out. When he smoked the tea bags it stunk the place out which didn't go down well with the rest of us. After a couple of warnings to stop it he was told that after tea he was doing the bed run. He was shitting himself, pleading for everyone to leave him alone but we packed our pillowcases with boots ready for the onslaught on this poor lad.

After being told twice, he started and everyone began laying into him. He was screaming to be left alone as he tried to carry on and as he went under the next bed, I was waiting with another lad to hit him with our stuffed pillowcases. Up he came and I hit him straight in the nose. It exploded with blood where my boot had hit him. He was laying on the bed at this point and I looked up and saw that two screws had come into the dorm. They came up to me and the other lad and said that we were both nicked for assault.

I was led out and placed in the punishment cell and told I would see the prison governor in the morning. I had no idea what would happen to me to me. In my eyes it was harmless fun and I had never meant to bust his nose open. I doubted the governor would share my views though. It was a long night in the cell with nothing but my thoughts and in the morning the door opened and I was handed breakfast and given a piece of paper which was my charge sheet and informed that I would be taken to see the governor at ten thirty.

I was escorted by a screw who told me to wait on the bench outside the office and after a few minutes the door opened and the other lad walked out. I was instructed to come in and to stand in front of the desk and give my name and number to the governor. Then, he looked at me and read out the charge. I was asked if I pleaded guilty or not guilty and I replied guilty. At this point I was told to sit down again whilst a screw gave his version of events.

I sat and listened to how the screw had heard a lot of shouting as he entered the dorm and saw me strike the lad in the face with a pillowcase. Case closed, guilty as charged. The governor told me to stand and asked me if I had anything to say before he passed sentence. I just said I was sorry and it would not happen again. I got seven days loss of remission, suspended for twenty-eight days. Then I was led out of the office and returned to the dorm.

The days started flying by. I was fit and healthy due to the amount of running we did, every day after work we had PE. This started with two laps of the fence that surrounded the football pitch, followed by a game of football. The prison had a team that played in the Stoke Sunday league. Whilst I was in there, I was picked to play along with Gaz. I was in Werrington House when the 1990 World Cup was being held in Italy. Everyone gathered around the television at the end of the dorm, cheering on

England until they got knocked out by Germany. My time was coming up. I had been inside for six weeks and I was due to be released on Friday 13th July 1990.

Gaz was due to be released in a month's time so we arranged to meet up in Macclesfield the day he got out. The night before I was released, I couldn't sleep. I was excited and nervous and didn't know what to expect when I got back home.

Mum and dad had told me that they would not be putting up with any more shit and I promised them that I had learned my lesson and I was going to find a job and keep my head down. I meant every word of what I said but it must have been a nightmare for my family having someone they loved in prison. It's only now when you look back that you try to understand how it must have been for them, the worry, the shame. It's something that I have to live with. The fact that I put them through this was unfortunately only the beginning. Things were going to get a lot worse.

Chapter 10- The Story of H.A.T and the Road to Hindley

Leaving Werrington House on that sunny Friday morning, I was apprehensive about returning home and not sure what to expect. I had every intention of putting all this behind me and making my family proud of me. There were three of us who were being released that day and all of us had the same aspirations of never returning to prison. That was the aim and I wonder if the guys that left Werrington with me that day ever returned.

    I climbed into the prison van that would take me to the train station so I could catch the train back home to Macclesfield. I arrived to be greeted by Rob and Skez. It was good to see them both and we all laughed as I told them what it was like inside as we walked to see our mate Wogger. He was still in bed but said he would come and meet us later. Rob said we were going to have a party to welcome me home. When we got to Hurdsfield Junior School the kids were playing in the yard, and I walked into the playground looking for my brother Danny. When I spotted him, I shouted him to come over and we spoke for a couple of minutes until a teacher came out asking who we were.

Then we went around the girls' house for a while and later I went home to see mum and dad. As you can imagine they were pleased to see me back home. They had hopes for me that soon evaporated when I announced that I was going back out. My dad wanted to know where I was going. I hadn't been home long so he couldn't understand why I wanted to go back out so soon. When I said I was off to see my mates, dad went mad, shouting at me and saying he was disappointed that I couldn't wait to see them and asking me they were when I was locked up. He had a point because I was pissed off with the fact that after everything I had done for Rob, he had only sent me one letter that everyone wrote together when they were pissed up. I was not going to agree with my dad though, even if I knew deep down, he was right.

The problem is at that young age and being in those circumstances, it was about loyalty to my mates and nothing my parents said could change the fact that I put my mates first. My family had been there for me, standing by me all through all of this but looking through my selfish eyes, my friends came first. I had been out of prison less than twelve hours and all my promises were sounding false.

I met up with the lads and we had a welcome party. It was good to be back with everyone and we all had a good time. A couple of weeks later Rob was due up at court for his charges. Ironically, Rob got sent down for a month. I should have seen it coming, the way Rob was behaving it was only a matter of time. I should not have taken the blame for him on that assault charge. He wasn't exactly thankful, looking back, and found himself in Werrington House. The day he was released from prison he was arrested for shoplifting from the Spar. He went into the shop pissed out of his head and stole four cans of Special Brew. He had only been out for about six hours.

Gary got released and came to Macclesfield to see me. The thing that I have always admired about Gaz is, the fact that he gave me his word that he would come and see me when he came out and he kept it. Gary has always been a good pal of mine. Our paths went in different directions and I wish him well but it's nice to see him when we meet up every now and then.

On the other side of town was a gang of lads who called themselves the Moss Rats. They were a lot older than I was and everyone had heard of them. They were well known around the town for causing mayhem like the rats that they were, picking on people. They always attacked at random like a baying mob. I first came across them when the fair came to town. I was stood near the waltzers when a bloke went running past me with about four or five lads chasing him. They grabbed hold of him and gave him a good kicking, leaving him lying on the floor unconscious. As they walked back towards me, they were congratulating themselves on a job well done. This was the first time I had seen the Moss Rats who, in the late 80s and early 90s, were a feared gang. Even now people from the Moss estate are referred to by their name.

On the Hurdsfield estate (or HField as the new generation call it) is a gang that calls themselves H.A.T. Depending on who you listen to, there are always stories about where the name H.A.T came from and who started it, with different generations all claiming to own the name. Fair play to them I say but it does make me smile when you hear these youngsters going around calling themselves H.A.T, making out that it's all down to them.

I am now going to set the record straight about what H.A.T stands for, who started it, who were the original members and how it came about in the first place.

Rob, Skez and me were sat round Skez's house one day watching the 1989 film The Firm about football hooligans, starring Gary Oldman and Phil Davis, amongst others. During this film there is a scene where Yeti drives a soft-top, Golf GTI across a football pitch. At this point Skez became obsessed with GTIs. The film is about three different, rival gangs of football hooligans who fight each other to determine who leads a national firm into the European Championships. Each firm had a name known to others and after watching this, we decided that we were going to call ourselves something, a bit like what the Moss Rats had done (God knows who came up with that name).

We sat around throwing a few names about when one of us shouted out "The Governors". This sounded good, then Rob said, "what about shorting it to the Guvs?". This sounded even better. We had been drinking and that added to the fact that we now had a gang name and began getting carried away with ourselves.

Rob then suggested we have Guvs tattooed on our arms with some Indian ink that he had. This sounded like a laugh, so after another drink Skez decided he would go first. Rob got the needle and started work on Skez's arm, I was laughing my head off as Rob was butchering Skez. Finally, he finished and after wiping all the blood away we looked at the finished masterpiece. It was alright but there was no way that I was doing the same. Rob had a go at trying to do his tattoo but soon gave up, in the end it was only Skez who had it done.

After a month or so we decided that the Guvs wasn't catching on so we started trying to come up with something different. We were sat outside the shops drinking, like we normally did, and talking about going to court. All three of us at this point were on bail for assault and as we were talking about this, I mentioned that we were the Hurdsfield Assault Team. We all laughed then stopped and just looked at each other and smiled. This was the point that we changed our name and started writing it on the walls at the shops, as well as the benches out front.

Hurdsfield Assault Team soon took off and people started talking about us, especially due to the way we were behaving around the shops. We were becoming a problem, intimidating people who were walking past, drinking every night. We thought and acted like we owned the place and if anyone said anything, we would start on them. The police were driving around a lot more taking an interest in us but we didn't give a fuck. We were getting a reputation as people to stay clear of. We thrived off it, playing up to the role and telling everyone knew who we were so they started to associate us with the label.

One night I was at the back of the shops where there was an old council depot. The gate was open so I went in to have a nosey. I found some white paint and a paint brush that had been left out, I picked it up and took it around to the front of the shops. Skez and Rob were sat there and I said I was going to write Hurdsfield Assault Team on the wall next to the paper shop, which had recently been painted black.

I did the letter H, then realised that I had painted it a bit too big and wouldn't be able to fit the rest on the wall. I was just about to leave it when Rob shouted to just put the initials. It just said HAT but didn't look quite right, so I went over and put a dot after the H and A. From that moment on we dropped Hurdsfield Assault Team and started calling ourselves H.A.T. Thirty years later people still mention it and the name is always associated with the youth of that estate.

Since I came out of prison my attitude had gotten worse. I was now starting to get a reputation as someone not to be messed with. This was coming to fruit before I got sent to prison, so now I was out of there I was actually thinking I was someone special. I was drinking all the time, not working so I signed on to the dole. Every two weeks, when I got my giro on the Thursday morning, I would cash it at the post office, then go straight to the shop and buy a load of alcohol. Come Saturday, I would be skint. I would avoid going home because it always ended in a row. I never once offered any money for my keep and would be offended if mum or dad so much as asked for anything towards the running of the house. I would lie when I had spent it all, saying that I hadn't received it yet. It never entered my head to offer up a couple of quid to help out. The thing is I would not have batted an eyelid if my mates wanted a bottle of cider or a few cans. I would buy them that without a second thought.

At this point I was sharing a bedroom with our Danny because Terry had taken my room when I was in prison. I was nasty with him, telling him to be quiet all the time, because I was lying in bed with a hangover and all Danny wanted to do was play with his toys. Danny was eight years younger than me so he was 10 at this point. I didn't have any time for Danny or anyone else for that matter. It was all about me and my needs. I was a self-centered and horrible, selfish bastard but I didn't care and just carried on.

It wouldn't be long before I was getting into trouble again with the police. All I was interested in was building my reputation and proving to everyone what a hard man I thought I was. I would do anything to cement that rep anyway possible.

It was around this time that I met Stephen in the summer of 1990. I had seen Ste around a few times but had never spoken to him. One night I was at the old market stalls with Rob and Skez, just sat around drinking, when a group of lads came walking over to us. In this group was Ste, and two brothers called Scott and Darren. We hit it off straight away and I am still friends with all three. We all started having a laugh together and soon after this meeting, I started knocking around with Ste a lot more. We became close and when we were together trouble was not far away.

We were on the same page in the sense that if anyone wanted a fight then they could have it. We both took it up to the next level with drinking and getting into trouble and were getting a reputation around the pubs of starting when we were pissed out of our heads. It began that every time I went out drinking, I would get into a fight with someone.

Macclesfield was becoming a violent town in the early 90s. After the pubs shut everyone would end up either at Waters Green or Park Green, depending on what pubs they had been in. You could guarantee that mass brawls would break out all over the town and this was starting to become the norm.

One night a lad started giving me shit outside the chippy. I didn't know him so I told him to fuck off and leave me alone. This only seemed to make him more agitated and the next thing I know is, he's coming towards me. I just punched him straight in the head, he fell to the floor and I gave him a good hiding. He finally got up and went home to lick his wounds and I went home and thought nothing more about it.

A week or so later I was sat around the shops, when Rob told me that a lad called Simon was looking for me, because I had battered his cousin the week before and he'd been telling everyone that when he saw me, he was going to do me in. I didn't know this Simon at all but what surprised me the most was all he had to do was walk up to the shops on the estate and nine times out of ten I would have been sat there. Instead he was telling everyone what he was going to do.

There was no way that I could let this go without doing anything so a couple of nights later I was with my mate John, when we saw a lad in front of the flats and John told me that the lad was Simon. I shot down the stairs and ran out of the flats to where I could see Simon walking along and shouted as I ran towards him. I was face to face with him when I asked if he was looking for me. He started going on that he just wanted to know what had happened with his cousin, that was all, I said "bollocks you told everyone that you were going to do me"! He denied this and started to walk away so I grabbed him and started hitting him. He tried to get away as I was punching him and finally shook me off and ran.

A couple of days later, early one morning, I was asleep in bed when I was woken up by my mum telling me that the police were at the door. I went downstairs to see them and was informed that I was under arrest for the assault on Simon. I honestly couldn't believe that someone who was telling everyone that he was going to do to me in, would go running to the police after being turned over. I was interviewed and charged with section 47 Assault and bailed to appear in court.

Not long after this I was arrested again, this time for assault and criminal damage. This was the same scenario because I had been told that a lad called Gerry was looking for me because someone told him that I had been seeing his girlfriend. This was untrue but that didn't stop him from telling people that he was looking for me.

I was out drinking with my mate Daz when I heard that Gerry was drinking in the Albion pub. I asked Daz to give me a lift to the Albion and once we got there, told him to wait outside. I walked in and saw Gerry stood near the bar and as soon as he saw me, we started fighting. A few of the locals in there joined in trying to get me out of the door and during the scuffle a window got smashed. Outside I jumped in the car and Daz drove off. I asked him to take me home and as soon as I walked through the front door, the police were there to arrest me on suspicion of assault and criminal damage.

My parents were in despair at my actions. Every time my dad went out for a pint in his local, someone was saying something about me and my dad couldn't defend me because he didn't know what I was doing all the time. The police charged me with criminal damage of the pub door but Gerry wouldn't press charges for assaulting him. Again, I was bailed to appear at court.

When I left the police station, I walked towards the George pub, and as I got nearer, I noticed that there was a door open at the back. There was no one about, but there were bottles and crates of lager and cider stacked up. I grabbed hold of a crate and walked down the hill towards home.

The following day I met up with Skez and Rob and showed them the beer that I had nicked and we sat around the back of the shops drinking the crate between us. With money in short supply this was an ideal situation. So, we could carry on drinking, we would sneak round the back of the George and take a couple of crates. We did this a few times without getting caught but one afternoon we were sat around the girls' house and Rob was pissed up when he announced that he was going up the George to get some more alcohol, we told him not to be so stupid as it was broad daylight and the pub was open. Rob was adamant that he was going, so off he went.

About an hour later a car pulled up outside the house and Rob came to the door with a car full of drink that he had just nicked. He had grabbed the crates and put them on the side of the road and then flagged a car down and delivered to us. Unbelievable looking back that he did that but at that time we just didn't care, it was a game to us.

Once me and Ste had a binbag full of bottles that we had taken from the George. We went to the top floor of Range Court Flats and drank the lot. Later, the police drove past us, then they stopped and reversed looking for Ste. When they pulled up Ste, who was totally pissed, just opened the back door of the police car and climbed in, passing out on the back seat. The police then drove off taking him to the nick.

Alcohol was becoming more of a problem for me. I was drinking more and more on a daily basis and the more I drank the more trouble I would find myself in. I was blacking out, not remembering a thing and when someone told me what I had done I would act like I wasn't bothered. Every penny that any of us had, we would pool together so we could get pissed or we would get someone to shoplift cans from the local Spar if we didn't have any money.

If I had my giro, I would pay some with Rob and Skez when they had theirs. We were in the Nag's Head one afternoon when Rob started arguing with the landlord, and we were told to leave. We started walking along Sunderland Street, when Rob spotted a BMX bike and jumped on it, riding off towards the old bus station. I shouted, telling him to put the bike back but Rob, thinking it was a laugh, refused so I grabbed him and pushed him off. We started arguing and I grabbed the BMX and threw it into the path of an oncoming car causing the driver to brake and hit it.

At this point a police car was travelling along the road towards where we were stood. They saw what I'd done and told us to stand against the wall while they spoke to the driver to see if he was alright. They then arrested all three of us and we were driven the short distance to the police station for questioning where I admitted to throwing the bike and got charged with criminal damage. Rob admitted taking the bike so he was charged with theft. Skez was released without charge. All this because we were drunk out of our tiny minds thinking it was funny.

The way things were going I was heading for a big fall. My dad tried to sit me down to talk to me but that would always end up in an argument before it started. I would refuse to sit down when he asked me to and this led to a full-scale row breaking out, with my mum standing between us. I would storm out and then the cycle would be repeated. I was drinking more and more, getting totally pissed of out of my mind at every opportunity and this led to me getting arrested by the police for stupid things that no sober person would even think of, never mind participating in.

My problem was that when I had a drink, I had to prove to the world that I was a somebody. I couldn't be seen backing down from anything. This has always caused me problems and one event that sticks out in my mind was the time that I was drinking outside the shops on Hurdsfield when I ran out of orange to mix with vodka. Without thinking I walked into the Spar and helped myself to a bottle of fresh orange and walked straight out without paying for it. Unbeknownst to me there was a plain clothes policeman in the shop who watched me do it. So off I went to the police station to be charged with theft of a 50p carton. Embarrassing really, seeing as I had money on me.

I kept this quiet from my parents when I went to court and received a conditional discharge and a fine. That was until the following Thursday when my dad was in the Flowerpot pub having a quiet pint and someone told him that I was in the local paper for this misdemeanor. Well, the next thing you know, I was sat in the Puss & Boots, when my dad flew through the door going mad at me, demanding that I get home.

When we got home the routine started, with my dad telling me to sit down, me refusing to tell him I am fine standing and mum going mad as my brothers looked on in disbelief. My dad couldn't understand what I was doing with my life and he couldn't understand why I was always getting into trouble. They were both looking at me for an explanation. I looked at them both, telling them I was just having fun and I will be fine.

Unbelievable really, seeing I had just completed a prison sentence and I was on bail for Assault and Criminal Damage. On top of this I had just been fined for nicking the orange juice. I was 18 years old and on the verge of alcoholism. In my mind I could not understand what was wrong with my mum and dad and it was at this point I said the words that would come back to haunt me. I told my bewildered parents that there was nothing to worry about as these were only Mickey Mouse charges, leaving my mum and dad open mouthed. I then went out to meet my mates again, getting pissed out of my head.

A few weeks later, one Saturday in October 1990 I met my mate Stephen for a day's drinking. We walked down to the Bear's Head for a few pints and were having a good time enjoying the day. We decided to go and have a walk about around a couple of different pubs, seeing who was out. It was getting to around five o'clock when we realised that we were running out of money. Ste said he would ask his mum for a borrow, so we both walked up to his house. He got some money and we called in to the Bramble pub which is outside Macc Town football club and sat down with our drinks.

It was early in there so it was quiet and I suggested going to the shop and buying a bottle of vodka and orange juice so we could have some cheap booze. Then we then started topping our glasses up with the vodka as we continued getting more drunk. A lad we knew called Brooksey came in, all suited and booted, got a drink and came over to join us. After a while Ste got up to go to the toilet and I put one of the orange cartons under his seat. Brooksey was sat facing him with a white shirt on, and as Ste came back and sat down carton exploded over Brooksey. Me and Ste just sat there laughing our heads off.

Soon we had finished the vodka and I went into the toilet with the bottle thinking that I had to hide it. I was looking around thinking what to do (when really all I had to do was put it behind the door or something) and I picked up the lid to the toilet cistern and put the bottle in. As I went to put the lid back on, I dropped it into the toilet bowl, smashing it and making the toilet flood. I came out and sat back down and Ste asked what the fuck the noise was. I told him, and how there was water all over the toile but the next thing I know is the bouncer on the door walks into the toilet then walks out holding the vodka bottle in his hand. He goes to the bar and the staff are all looking over to where me and Ste are sat. I thought to myself 'here we go'.

The bouncer walked over to me and asked who put the bottle in the toilet and smashed it up. I stood up telling him to fuck off and then headbutted him before trying to get out of the pub through the back near the football pitch. The bouncer followed me trying to get me back and we were fighting all the way back inside. I turned around and seen there was about four policemen walking into the pub. I knew that I was in the shit but I was out of control and drunk out of my head and I didn't care. At this point I blacked out I didn't know what I was doing.

The police came towards me and I punched the first one who went down and the next one grabbed me so I headbutted him. I attacked another police officer during the struggle to handcuff me and they finally got the cuffs on and me into the van.

I hadn't finished at this point as I was struggling to attack the policemen in the back of the van despite being under arrest, handcuffed and restrained. The Black Maria was rocking all the way to the police station and I was dragged into the station kicking and shouting obscenities. I was placed straight in the drunk cell and the handcuffs were removed and I collapsed, passing out on the bed.

Chapter 11- A Trip to Hell and Back

I opened my eyes and looked around and the familiar dreaded feeling engulfed my stomach. I had no recollection of what had happened the night before but I knew I was in trouble. I rang the bell to ask for a drink as my mouth was dry and was passed a cup of water and told that I would be taken to see the desk sergeant to be formally booked in as I had been in no fit state to go through the process last night due to my behaviour. At this point I knew I was in the shit; the only problem was I didn't know what I had actually done.

I was taken to the bench where the sergeant informed me that I had been arrested on suspicion of criminal damage to the toilet of the Bramble pub, suspicion of assault on the pub bouncer, and suspicion of three assaults on police. There was also suspicion of criminal damage to the police van. My heart sank. I could not believe what was being said nor remember anything.

I asked for a solicitor before being placed back into my cell where I had a lot to think about.

A couple of hours later I was taken to meet my solicitor who explained what he had been told by the witness statements and it did not look good for me. I told him what I could remember from the day and night. That I remembered being in the Bramble, drinking the vodka with Ste and that was about it. I had no recollection of anything else and was advised to say no comment during interview.

I was interviewed and answered 'no comment' to every question. When it was concluded I was taken back to my cell and a short while later the solicitor came to see me again. He informed me that they we are looking at charging me with three police assaults and criminal damage to the pub toilet. The assault on the bouncer had been dropped, as had the criminal damage to the prison van. He informed me that the police were opposing bail because I was, by now, on bail already for four assaults and two criminal damage charges. He said I would see him at the magistrates court the following morning where he would try and get me bail then.

After a long sobering night in the cells I was taken by police car to the magistrates court on Park Green, only this time it was through the back entrance. I was placed in a holding cell and the solicitor arrived and we went to a small room where he explained that they were looking at remanding me to custody. He explained that because I had committed similar offences to the ones that I was on bail for, the prosecution thought (and rightly so) that I would reoffend. I wasn't surprised by what he told me and the fact that every time I went out, I was either fighting or getting arrested for something stupid should have set alarm bells ringing. I had never been remanded before but I knew that it would not be the soft approach that Werrington was. I was led handcuffed into the dock by the court officers and I noticed that this time there was no fanfare like before. I was well and truly on my own. My parents were working so they would not be attending, not that I expected them to. When they found out I had been arrested they were, as you can imagine, at the end of their tether. There were no mates rooting for me at the back of the court as I looked around. It was nearly empty, except for a couple of people sat at the back who I didn't know. Someone from the Macclesfield Express who looked at me with a pen in his hand ready to tell the townsfolk about who had been naughty.

I was asked my name and address then told to sit down. The prosecutor outlined the offences and the fact that I was already on bail for an assault and criminal damage. My solicitor then addressed the bench but it was pointless. I was remanded into custody for seven days and led back into the holding cell. The solicitor came to see me to tell me that he was sorry and I asked him what happens now because I had never been in this position before. He explained that I would return to court next week and he would try again to apply for bail. In the meantime, I would be taken to a prison for the week. My solicitor asked the court guards who informed him that I would be going to Hindley prison which I learned was near Wigan.

I waited in the holding cell for a couple of hours until the morning court had finished and a short time later a prison van came to collect me. It must have stopped at every court in Cheshire on its way to Hindley and by the time we arrived it was full of people who had been remanded or sentenced. When we arrived at Hindley, we were led into a big holding area which had benches all around the wall. There were people who had been brought in from all over Cheshire, North Wales, Liverpool and the Manchester areas.

I had been there about five minutes when I saw a lad go over to another and ask him what size trainers he was wearing. He is wearing a new pair of Reeboks. The lad said "what?!!" so the lad repeated himself. He said size 9s so the other lad told him to take them off, I was sat there transfixed by what I was watching, I could not believe what I was seeing. It was funny on one hand but on the other I was on edge with what was going on. The lad said no so he grabbed him and made him hand them over. The guy then walked over to the bench, casually sat down and took his shitty pair of trainers off and put the lads new Reebok on. He then tossed the shitty pair to the lad who was sat there in his socks and told him to put them on, which he did. This is what is known as taxing. I had just seen first-hand that if you did not mark your card in prison you were fucked.

I knew that this was going to be totally different from the stint I had already served and I would have to be on my guard at all times. You may ask what would I do in that situation. I would smack him first and worry about the consequences later. The minute you give in then you are in for a hard time because word will get around that you are a soft touch.

Back in the holding cell it was getting more and more packed with new arrivals, then I heard my name being called so I walked over to a door where a screw was stood. He asked me my name then he led me into the reception. Because I was on remand I was kitted out and taken to D wing. The first thing I noticed when I arrived on the wing was the noise. It was loud and everything seemed to be going at 100mph, even though everyone was banged up. There was a group of us who were taken to the main office on the wing, on the first-floor landing known as the 1s. In Hindley there was four landings on each wing with two spurs on each landing. I was then allocated a single cell on the 2s where I was banged up. In my cell there was nothing except a bed and a table and chair and there was a smell of piss coming from under the bed. I bent down and saw what looked like a small bucket with a lid next to it. I pulled it out and could not believe the smell. It was half full of piss and it smelled that bad I thought I was going to be sick. I looked around and soon realised that there was nowhere to tip it. I put the lid back on it which got rid of a bit of the smell, made my bed up and lay down listening to everyone shouting out of the windows to their mates.

A couple of hours later the door opened and a screw shouted, "Slop out then get your tea". I grabbed the bucket then followed the crowd who were all carrying the same thing. I realised that this was where we had to go if we needed the toilet and it stayed in our cells day and night and were affectionately known as a piss pot. I emptied mine in the sink in the recess then went down to where tea was being served. I got my food on a metal tray and was told to return to my cell to eat it.

I was now sat in a cell that stank of piss from my heavily stained piss pot that had been festering God knows how long and was expected to eat my meals in there as well.

About an hour later I was told to put my tray outside the door, then offered a cup of tea out of an urn that was being dragged along by a kitchen orderly. Then it was bang up until the following morning. I just lay down on my bed trying to ignore the smell. I had literally nothing in my cell. I had nothing to read and there was nothing to do except lie there.

After a while I could hear someone banging on my ceiling, then shouting for me to go to the window. I ignored it at first but they just carried on until I stood at the window and asked him what he wanted. He asked me to pass him some burn. I said I didn't smoke so he called me a liar and told me not to be shady. I shouted back I did not have any burn so he then asked me to sing him a song out of the window. I replied that I didn't sing either and he then started going mad, banging on the ceiling, shouting out of the window that in the morning he was going to rip my head off. I just lay back down, listening to him telling the whole of D wing what he was going to do to me. This carried on for a short while until he started on someone else. What made me laugh was the fact that I knew nobody in there yet a total stranger was going to come in my cell in the morning and rip my head off because I didn't smoke and wouldn't sing for his entertainment.

No one came the next morning or any morning after that. It was all bullshit and bravado behind a door to make himself out to be somebody he wasn't. I am not saying that I wasn't shitting myself because I was. Not because I felt threatened from some stranger in the cell above me for not being a performing seal. It was fear of the unknown. I had only been in there a few hours and I could see how violent the place could be. You had a load of lads from all across the north west aged between 17 to 21, full of testosterone thinking they were ten men. I was in there on my own, banged up for twenty-three hours a day with nothing to do except lie there and listen to people threatening each other from out of there windows.

They always reeled someone in. I would be laying on my bed listening to someone getting threatened for hours on end until they cracked and then it one of two ways. The poor soul would either crack or ring his bell for a screw, who would arrive to be confronted by a lad crying his heart out, begging to be let out. At this point everyone would rip into him even more or they would stand at the window singing songs all night. Either way, they were in for a rough ride and that's why I would not allow myself to be a victim. You had to stand your ground from the start.

The week went slowly before I found myself back at Macclesfield magistrates. I was hopeful to be granted bail but unfortunately, I was remanded for another seven days and transported back to the madness of Hindley. I was placed back in the same single cell, with nothing to do for another week except twenty-three hours, banged up on my own.

When I was sat in the holding area, waiting to be taken back to the wing, there were only about twenty-five or thirty people in there. I was just sat there minding my business when a lad got up and walked over to where the first person was sat. He had a brown paper bag and he gestured to the lad to put something in there, which he did. He then started making his way along the line, taking things from each person. He got to a couple of people before me, when we were called to be taken through. I could feel my hands shaking with adrenaline because he was getting nothing from me. We were led back to D wing and his time I was placed in a cell with another lad. He was laying on the top bunk sweating and he looked a mess. The first thing he asked me was if I had any gear on me (heroin). I said I didn't take drugs. Then he said his name was Taffy and he was from Birkenhead. He was in a bad way, on remand and days into withdrawal from heroin. He looked and smelt like shit.

I spent the next three days padded up with him and it was the worst and longest three days in my life. Taffy should have been on the hospital wing not lying on the top bunk above me

We were locked up for twenty-three hours a day and each passing hour felt like a lifetime. The first night I lay on the bottom bunk listening to Taffy moan and cry as the withdrawal kicked in properly. I had just fallen asleep when I felt the bed frame start shaking. I got up and looked at Taffy, sweating and full-on shaking on the bed. I asked him if he were OK and he said he needed some gear and then he would be alright. Unfortunately, he couldn't get any and I got little sleep due to the amount of shaking he was doing. The following day Taffy was in a right state, begging the screws to see the doctor. They told him that the doctor would be round later that day. He was pleading with them but they just shut the door. The doctor never came and that day was one of the longest I have ever known. Taffy had been sick in the piss pot a couple of times, which had been emptied but the problem was he was feeling sick and was starting to get diarrhoea. This wasn't a problem until after tea when everyone was banged up for the night.

Now, bearing in mind that in Hindley you had your tea at about 4.00 o'clock, it was a hell of a long time until breakfast the following morning, to be locked in a cell with only a piss pot between you, especially when one of you is going cold turkey and is throwing up and wants to shit at the same time.

Taffy was in bed shaking like a kitten, his bed sheets were piss-wet through with sweat as he tossed and turned. I was praying that I could get some sleep. When I finally did, I was woken up by a strong smell of shit, followed by a dripping noise. Taffy had shit his bed and it had dripped down on to my bunk then onto the floor. I jumped up, switched on the light and I couldn't believe what I was seeing. Taffy was asleep, lying in his own diarrhoea, the smell was unbelievable. I didn't want to wake him, so I cleaned up my bed and the floor the best I could and spent the rest of the night sat on the chair trying to survive the night.

The following morning when the screws opened the door. I told the screw that Taffy needed the hospital wing. He looked at the state of the cell and told me to slop out. He left and returned about ten minutes later, telling me to get my stuff as I was moving cells.

After three weeks of being on remand I was back in court where I pleaded guilty to all charges against me and the case was adjourned for pre-sentence reports from the probation service. My solicitor applied for bail with conditions attached and after a lengthy debate with the magistrates I was granted conditional bail and placed on a curfew where I had to be indoors between 7.00pm and 7.00am. I was also banned from all licenced premises in Macclesfield which meant I couldn't go to the pub or in any shop that sold alcohol. I was only glad to get out of Hindley and after the experience with Taffy, I never wanted to see that place again. Little did I know that this was only the starter, the main course and desert would soon be on their way.

I was due back in court in four weeks with no guarantees of not returning to prison. Under a curfew, living at my parents and I had just had the worst experience of my life, you would have thought I would be sorting myself out but the following Saturday I went out for a walk around town just for something to do. At about two o'clock I decided to head back home and bumped into Rob. He was half pissed, carrying a bag full of alcohol. He offered me a can and I thought that having a couple wouldn't hurt anyone and I'd still be home for seven o'clock. Unfortunately, that can turned into me getting absolutely pissed out of head and drinking a bottle of vodka.

I finally got home sometime after seven o'clock. Mum and dad were furious with me, disgusted with me and my behaviour and rightly so. I couldn't be trusted to go for a walk around town without coming home in a complete state. The fact that I had just spent three weeks on remand had gone out of the window. I was late home, breaking my curfew and on top of that I was drunk out of my mind. I just didn't care though. I had no thought or consideration for anyone but myself. My mum was screaming at me to sort myself out and then I exploded. I started swearing at my parents, asking them who did they think they were, telling me what to do. I was totally disrespectful to them both and told them that I was going back out. My dad said that I wasn't, so I asked him if he was going to stop me. I then ran off and headed down Dunster Road with dad running after me. I was so pissed that I didn't get very far and he dragged me back home. I refused to go inside the house and stood in the front garden screaming abuse at everybody. I then picked up a big stone from the garden wall and threatened to throw it straight through our front room window. I was totally out of control and by now the neighbours were on the street wondering what the commotion was.

I then decided that I was going to climb on the bungalow roof that faced our house. I got up there and was threatening to throw myself off. All a bit pathetic really seeing it was only two metres high. My mum was screaming at me to get down but I refused. This went on until I started walking and slipped and fell off the roof, landing on the grass. The next thing I remember is waking up the following morning with a hangover from hell and no recollection of what had happened the previous night. I had (not for the first time blacked out, as you can imagine my family was disgusted with me. All I could do was apologise, which they had heard a hundred times before, the minor miracle in all this was how on Earth the police had not been called because if they had, it would have been straight back to Hindley with even more charges. For that small fortune I am grateful.

I returned to Macclesfield magistrates for sentencing and this time the court followed the probations recommendation and I was sentenced to 160 hours of community service. I also had to attend a probation course on alcohol awareness along with a compensation order for the criminal damage. In the circumstances, an incredibly good result seeing what I had been charged with.

Things had been going well for me. I had been staying out of trouble and keeping my head down until one night that changed everything. It was very nearly my last night ever. It was a normal, quiet Thursday night and I was having a few beers with my mate Earlsey in the Jolly Sailor. We decided to head to another pub, finished our drinks and headed out. I then saw two lads walking towards us. I didn't know either but Earlsey knew one of them and they started arguing. I then noticed that one of them had a knife and I shouted to Earlsey to leave it. We both turned to walk away, when I suddenly felt a blow to the back of my head and turned around ready to confront the lad who did it. I felt something trickle down the back of my head and put my hand to where I had been struck and it was covered in blood. I realised he had stabbed me and, as I turned to walk away, he lunged and stabbed me in the backside. I tried to carry on walking but blood was now gushing out of the back of my head and my jeans were turning red. A taxi driver who knew me came over to help and phoned an ambulance, as I collapsed on the pavement. I was taken to Macclesfield general hospital where I went straight into surgery to stitch my wounds up before I lost too much blood

My parents were at my bedside along with the police who had arrested the lad who did it. They wanted a statement and at first, I refused but my parents were fuming, telling me I was lucky to be alive and this lad was known for doing what he had done to me. So, I made a statement to the police. I had not even said a word to either the guy or his mate and I certainly hadn't been looking to get involved in anything with them. I know Earlsey was having words with him but that was nothing to do with me. It was an unprovoked attack involving a knife that could have killed me. An inch or two was all it would have taken and I would not be here now.

The man who stabbed me got sentenced to four years in prison. The mad thing about all this was, at the time, me getting stabbed enhanced my reputation as it was all over town what had happened and in my eyes that was a good thing.

Chapter 12 – Running Riot With the Peel Street Boys

As I have mentioned, in the early 1990s Macclesfield was a violent town. There would be fights kicking off all over, every weekend. On a Friday night everyone used to end up in a bar called Ruben Stubbs and you could guarantee that someone would be kicking off in there. When that shut everyone used to congregate around Park Green. Running battles were frequent after the pubs had shut. Saturday nights would be spent at the top end of town and the pubs would be rammed. Then everyone would then go on to a club called Harlequins.

Harlequins at the time was the place to be, situated on two levels. You could stay downstairs and drink and dance, but upstairs was where the DJ was and you had to pay to go upstairs so that was the place to be. I used to always be up there with Ste and Mark and I used to mither the DJs to play KLF, Last Train to Tran Central. In the end, as soon as they saw that I was in, they would play it for me so I wouldn't keep asking them. I had some great nights in there but trouble would always be brewing. Before you knew it, a fight would break out and the bouncers would be wading in trying to restore order. One night me and Earlsey were walking down the stairs and there was a lad at the bottom shouting "I want you!" in our direction. As we got level with him, he smashed a bottle of beer in my face. I left and went to the Chestergate pub and, after a couple of minutes, this lad walked in so I just cracked him, knocking his teeth straight out in the process. He was dragged outside by the bouncers with his teeth missing. I had glass in my face and it took a couple of weeks to get it all out although luckily, I hadn't been scarred for life.

I had now been stabbed and bottled all in the space of a few months. When the pubs and clubs shut everyone would head to Waters Green where there were a couple of takeaways. You could guarantee that this is where it always kicked off. One minute you would be eating your supper, and the next you were rolling around the floor. It was becoming the norm for people in Macclesfield back then

Not far from the town centre, there was a pub called The Peel Arms. This pub was occupied by a group of lads called the Peel Street Boys. It was their local, where they always congregated before they hit the town. The thing with these boys was the fact that they were always out mob handed every weekend in a group which meant that everyone knew who they were. If trouble kicked off you could guess that they would be involved in it. They had a pack mentality and if you had a falling out with one of them, you could guarantee that you would end up fighting with them all. It was inevitable that mine and their paths would cross before too long.

I first became aware of who they were in Ruben Stubbs. About fifteen of them came in, taking the place straight over and before too long a fight had broken out and a few of them were in the middle of it battering someone. They had a reputation of dishing out beatings for next to nothing and one night after the pubs had shut, I ended up fighting with one of them. I can't remember what it was over, probably nothing knowing me. Anyway, it didn't last long and there was no damage done or so I thought. The following night I was in town when I heard that the Peel Street Boys were looking for me, mob handed as normal, over what had gone on the previous night. I was in Harlequins with my mate Mark when they came in and a couple of them came over, including the lad I was fighting with the previous night, trying to intimidate me. They said that I was going to get my head kicked in for starting on one of them, I knew that I was going to get it but I thought that I stood a better chance inside the pub instead of outside. At that point Mark came over to even up the odds and they walked off leaving us standing there. I knew that this wouldn't be the end of the matter by a long way.

The following week I was in back in Ruben Stubbs and I bumped straight into them. I was punched so I returned the punch and then I was set upon by all of them. The next thing that I knew, I was being picked up off the floor outside with my shirt ripped off my back. I had a few cuts and bruises but luckily that was all. The one thing I do remember is that as I was trying to get up one of them had kicked me in the head. I saw who it was, a lad who lived on the Hurdsfield estate.

The following week after a night out, I was walking with Mark towards his mum's house, when we could hear someone running towards us. As I turned around, I couldn't believe it. It was only the lad who kicked me in the head He came up, acting pleased to see us, like we were long lost pals.

I grabbed him and said that I had seen him kick me in the head but he denied it. I knew full well it was him and then he said that he was there but never joined in, you know the story. Anyway, he got battered by me and Mark for what he did.

After that it was getting tit for tat between me and them boys. Every time we saw each other something would happen. I wasn't scared of them, one on one I would always back myself but with the Peel Street Boys that was never the case. One night I met up with a lad called Stuart who was telling me that he was sick of the Peel Street Boys. He had had a few run-ins with them and was fed up that every time he went out, he would end up fighting with them. We hatched a plan that involved me, Stuart, another lad called Spam and Spam's girlfriend.

The plan was that we would walk into The Peel Arms the following Saturday night, arriving before they got in there and give it to them, and Spam's girlfriend would have a baseball bat hidden down her coat to even the odds. It seems crazy when I think back to this event. The pub was definitely a place that if you weren't invited you should stay clear of, yet here we were talking about going in there and ambushing them, madness really.

The following Saturday I was nervous. I wasn't sure if we would actually go through with it. I met up with Stuart at his flat and when I walked in, I was surprised to see Spam and his girlfriend sat there. I thought they may have had second thoughts but I was wrong, it was on. After a couple of drinks to calm the nerves, we set off. The plan was to get in there for about half six because we knew that they started meeting up about seven. When we arrived at the pub, I walked in first followed by the rest. The pub was empty and we found a table next to the door and ordered half a larger each and waited. Just after seven the door opened and they started walking in, a few at a time. When they got to the bar they turned and saw us and they couldn't believe it. After a few minutes they came over and asked us what we were doing in there. I just said we was having a quiet drink but they said, bollocks what's going on. Stuart just told them that we were sick of all this. Every weekend something was going on between us so enough was enough. To my surprise they agreed and we called a truce. We left our drinks and walked out with the baseball bat still under the coat, unused.

From that day until now I never had another cross word with any of them and soon, I was friends with them all. Even now, all these years later I go out drinking with them all and I am pleased that we all get on really well. At the end of the day it was all over nothing in the first place, too much ego and testosterone knocking about. When I talk to them over a few beers, we laugh about the things we got up to back in the day. Around about this time I was knocking about with Stephen and Mark, I have always been close to Mark's family growing up and we always spent a lot of our time down at their sister

Jackie's flat. When I was locked up in prison, Jackie always used to write to me and send me the odd postal order for which I was grateful.

Mark was always up to something and ne night he pulled up in a car and shouted to me to get in. It was obvious that it was nicked but we were just having a laugh. Mark was ragging it down the Silk Road when he went around the roundabout at Tesco's and he was going that fast that he drove us straight into the wall. We decamped and ran off leaving the car smoking in the middle of the road. I wasn't into nicking cars mainly because it's not my scene and I couldn't drive back then. Saying that though, I have been in a few nicked cars joyriding around the hills. It was seen as having a laugh. It seemed harmless at the time but obviously it wasn't. I was young and stupid in them days. We used to grab the car stereos and sell them on when we had no money to go out on the piss. If we were skint we would go out and grab a couple of stereos and that was us out on the town. I have never really been in to the whole going out committing burglaries or stealing, I know it sounds like I am contradicting myself and I did steal some car stereos and rode around in stolen cars from time to time, but they were few and far between and even though it was wrong, I never saw it that way at the time.

If I were on my own, I would have never dreamed of doing anything like that. When I was with Ste and Mark, I would join in thinking it would be a laugh. I never thought of the consequences or how what we did affected people. When you're young you think you're invincible. You never think further from your own nose.

I was once arrested for being in a stolen car. I was with Earlsey and we borrowed this car off a lad that had nicked it a few days before. We were drunk when it seemed a good idea to borrow this car, and we ended up on Hurdsfield estate when the police stopped us and everyone got arrested. Luckily for me we weren't charged with taking the car, we were all charged with allowing ourselves to be carried in a stolen vehicle. Earlsey was charged with drink driving as well.

Not long after this I was caught with Stephen in possession of couple of car stereos that we had just nicked. We were on our way to sell them when we got caught and the police took us both to Macclesfield police station for questioning. I gave a 'no comment' interview and was placed back in the cell. However, unknown to me, the police had got a search warrant to search my home.

I was still living with mum and dad at this point, and they were horrified when the police knocked on the door waving a search warrant looking for stolen car stereos. They searched my bedroom and the garden shed before leaving empty handed. Not that they would have found anything because as soon as we had nicked the stereos they were sold on. My parents yet again were in despair and now they had the police searching the house. The charges were building up again and I was on bail for being in the car. I was also charged with the car stereos. I had also taken a load of other car stereos that the police had taken into consideration.

I was running wild doing stupid things bringing shame to my family. All I was interested in was going out getting pissed. That's the only reason I got involved with the car stereos, because it was easy money. We knew someone who would buy as many as we could get our hands on, so every time we were skint we would nick a couple. After I was charged by the police I never did it again, it didn't seem worth it anymore, especially after they had searched my parents' house and I was on very thin ice with mum and dad. I was still going out all weekend getting into fights and my reputation was growing. It seemed that everyone was looking to fight me and at that time I was only happy to oblige. You could guarantee that, nine times out of ten, I would either end up in a fight or in the cells, no two ways about it. The thing was, at the time I wasn't bothered, I was going around doing what I wanted thinking I was having a good time, when in reality I was being a completely selfish prick. No one could tell me anything because I thought I knew everything.

The Mickey Mouse charges were stacking up again and prison was on the horizon, yet all I could think about was myself and my reputation. What happened next still troubles me. Earlsey and myself totally overstepped the mark and still to this day, I don't know how we didn't spend years in prison. We would have had no complaints if we got ten years each.

We were walking through the flats in Macclesfield when we bumped into this lad. Words were exchanged and we both gave this lad an absolutely vicious beating for no real reason. We kicked him senseless all up and down the flat. He was in an absolute mess when we left him, in a pool of blood unconscious. At one point we were going to throw him over the balcony and if that had happened, we would have killed him and most probably still would have been in prison now.

I feel uncomfortable writing about this, looking back at when it happened. I would have had no remorse whatsoever; it was a totally unprovoked attack where we could have killed this lad yet we were not bothered in the slightest.

About a month later early one morning, I was in bed at my mum and dad's house, when there was an almighty knocking at the door. I looked out of the window and could see police cars outside. Mum opened the door to be greeted by a CID officer asking for me. I was told to get dressed as I was being arrested for a serious assault. The CID officers waited downstairs with my mum and my brothers were just sat there wondering what on Earth I had been up to. I told them not to worry and I would see them later. Downstairs, I was formally arrested for a section eighteen, assault wounding with intent charge. The CID officer told me in the car that I had done it now. I was getting years for this one and so was Earlsey. I just looked out of the window as we made our way to the police station. They had arrested Earlsey that morning as well.

At the station, I asked to see my solicitor who soon arrived and I told him what had gone on, along with the fact that we both knew the bloke who had been assaulted. I had seen the lad in Morton Hall a few weeks after the assault and although he was still recovering, we spoke and I apologised to him for what I'd done. He wasn't happy but things were left there. My solicitor advised me to go 'no comment' all the way which I did. The CID weren't happy but they still charged us both with GBH. They also wanted us both locked up but we were back out on the streets carrying on the same as before.

It wouldn't be long before I was involved in fighting again. I was drinking in the Jolly Sailor in Macclesfield and was drunk as usual enjoying the night when I overheard a couple of lads talking between themselves about me, saying does the other lad know me etc. I then heard him say something about my grandad Costello and then they both started laughing looking in my direction. I was stewing but decided to leave it as I was having a good night but later that evening, I was walking towards Macclesfield train station when I saw one of the lads. I was well drunk at this point and in my head, I wasn't having him disrespecting me or my family. I pulled him and asked him what he had been saying. At first, he denied it but when I wasn't going to let it go, he surprised me by admitting that he said I was a pisshead just like my grandad. I saw red and started punching him but he managed to run off up the road. I couldn't believe what he'd said about my grandad. He later claimed that he was having a laugh and maybe if I was sober, I would have seen it that way but I didn't.

Unknown to me, he went to the police and made a statement saying that I had attacked him for no reason. I was again arrested and charged with section forty-seven assault. Luckily, I was again bailed and my solicitor had the task of getting the cases adjourned so they could all be tried together except the section twenty GBH which would be getting sent to the crown court.

During all this I was getting a lot of threats and intimidation from the family of the man who had stabbed me. They lived next door to my uncle Jimmy and if I saw any of them on the estate or around town, they would start with the threats. When I ignored all that then they tried to intimidate me but that didn't work either. It's not that I wasn't worried, I just knew that it was all words and if something were going to happen then it already would have in my opinion. I just stayed out of their way which was easier.

It was a different story with the lad who stabbed me though. Every time we saw each other it looked like it would kick off straight away, which it did in spectacular style one night between me and

Earlsey versus him and his mate. This turned into a running battle outside the Mulberry Bush pub.

We had been drinking in the Bush when we decided that we had enough in there so we were going to walk down the road to the Durham Ox. As we were leaving a car was driving past when it screeched to a halt. At that point, the lads in the car were staring at us, so me and Earlsey shouted to them to come on then if they wanted it. As we went towards them, the driver (the one who'd stabbed me) drove the car at us. He was revving the engine, trying to intimidate us both but that was never happening. I picked up a concrete slab from the car park wall and threw it at the car, hitting the side panel. Earlsey followed suit and this time his went straight through the back window. The driver started driving off so we ran after them, shouting at them to come on. It stopped at the green and they both jumped out of the car and opened the boot and the driver grabbed a shovel and ran at us swinging it. Me and Earlsey jumped on him and started punching and kicking him and his mate started swinging punches at us. It was a free for all, the four of us fighting with each other which was bringing a lot of attention with everyone coming out of their houses to see what the commotion was. We weren't bothered though and, as the fight continued, I grabbed the shovel and ran at the driver's mate. I missed the target as the lad ducked out of the way then dropped it and punched him, knocking him to the floor. After a few punches and kicks he was knocked out near the kerbside.

Everyone was screaming for us to stop but I wanted my revenge. The lad who had stabbed me was trying to get into his car to get away, so we started smashing it up, trying to break the windows as he tried to drive off. His mate was now trying to get off the floor and, in the car, so Earlsey ran over and jumped on his arm. You could hear it snap and the lad screamed as he got in and they sped away. The night had started with a few quiet drinks but ended in a full-scale riot.

The air was alive with sirens as the police raced to the scene and we were all arrested and charged with causing an affray. At the time it was a serious charge, the one above it is violent disorder and above that riot which carries a ten-year maximum prison sentence. It wasn't long before I was heading back to prison.

Looking back, I was out of control. My reputation was going before me and not in a good way. Earlsey was on remand in Hindley and it wouldn't be long before I was joining him. The charges were getting more serious and I was looking at a few years in prison. It was all deserved and it was early 1991. I wouldn't see much of daylight until 1992.

Chapter 13 – On the Merry Go Round

I had only been out of Hindley for about five months, when I breached my community services order and was sent back to court. This was on top of the charges that I was already on bail for so the courts decided enough was enough and I was remanded into custody. I had breached a community service order for police assaults and added at least a dozen more charges involving violence as well. It was only February 1991, just little over seven months later, and things weren't looking good for me at all.

I arrived back in Hindley and was put onto A wing which was where Earlsey who got there a couple of weeks earlier was. I met up with him the following morning in the exercise yard and when he saw me, he started laughing. It was good to see him as we had both known we would end up in there together at some point. Earlsey had got to know a few of the lads on his landing. They were and are good lads who are doing well for themselves now.

They were padded up together a few doors down from Ste.

The following week I was taken back to court with Earlsey to get a date for the GBH charges that we both faced and a date was arranged for a couple of weeks ahead. As we were both pleading not guilty, I now had a new solicitor who had requested a Newton hearing. A Newton hearing is a legal procedure where the two sides (defence and prosecution) offer such conflicting evidence that a magistrate sitting alone decides if there is enough evidence to take it to trial or whether to dismiss the charges.

When we got back to Hindley, I asked the screw on the way to A wing if I could get padded up with Earlsey, as we were co-accused. He said yes, so I moved into Ste's pad. Soon we were back to the magistrates court for the hearing. We both knew that if this went against us and it went to Crown court for trial, then we could be looking at five years, at least, for GBH so there was a lot at stake here.

We were led into the court room to be greeted by our friends and families who had come out to support us. There was a sense of excitement in the air as well as a nervousness of what might be ahead of us. The prosecution started to outline their case and the facts they said were that it was a totally unprovoked attack by two violent offenders and only by the grace of God, was it not a charge for murder. The prosecutor carried on painting a picture that, from my point of view wasn't looking good at all. There were gasps from our friends and families at the back of the court as the facts were presented, followed by the smirks from the police who thought they were going to have me and Ste off the streets of Macclesfield for a very long time. I was fearing the worst and when I looked at Earlsey I could tell he was feeling the same. The court was adjourned for lunch and after, the prosecution star witness, the lad who had been assaulted was going into the witness box. I certainly knew the writing was on the wall when our solicitor told us what we already knew. That there had been talk of pleading guilty to a lesser charge, but that had been rejected by the police and the prosecution. They had smelled blood and now they were going in for the kill.

When we walked back into the courtroom the atmosphere was different. There was tension in the air, a black cloud over the court. The lad was led into the dock and he looked at me and

Earlsey and winked at us. I glanced at Ste and said, "what was that about?". Ste didn't have a clue but we soon found out. What happened in the next hour were some of the most unbelievable scenes I think I have ever witnessed, never mind being a part of.

From the start he was abrupt and uncooperative with the prosecutor. When they asked him a question, he would be evasive, giving one word replies while we were sat there not quite believing what was going on. The mood had changed, there was a door opening but would there be enough to walk through? We would soon find out in spectacular style.

The prosecutor produced a photo album, containing photos of the lad after he had been assaulted that the police had taken for evidence. These were passed around the court for everyone to look at and I must admit, they were really bad. The prosecutor asked the lad to look at the photos and could he confirm that this was him. He said no, it wasn't. I couldn't quite believe what I was hearing and neither could my solicitor. The prosecutor continued. "What do you mean that isn't you?", to which the lad replied again that it wasn't him. There were gasps of amazement from around the courtroom. Then the prosecutor asked him if he had been assaulted by the defendants, to which he replied that no it wasn't me or Earlsey that had assaulted him and that we were friends of his. The prosecutor and the police were lost for words.

Our solicitor stood up and asked to see the magistrate along with the prosecutor. The court was cleared and we were taken back into the cells while they discussed what was going on. We never expected that and even the screws who had escorted us both said they had never heard of anything like this.

After a while Ruth came to see us with news. The prosecution case against us had fallen apart and the prosecution was now looking at a deal. Instead of the section twenty, we could plead guilty to a lesser assault charge of section forty-seven and get dealt with today. I asked her what she thought and she said that with the victim adamant it wasn't us that had assaulted him, there was no chance of any conviction. The prosecution was desperate for any result which was why now they wanted a deal. We all decided to refuse the deal and ask for the case to be thrown out.

We were led back into court where the atmosphere was totally different again. There were a lot a smiles from our families and friends with the police looking absolutely gutted. Our solicitor asked the court that, in light of the new developments, to dismiss the charges against us due to lack of evidence. The magistrate asked the prosecution if they had anything to add, which they didn't so the case was dismissed. I couldn't believe what had happened. It was certainly a relief, as we said our goodbyes to our friends and families to be taken back to Hindley (as we were on remand for other offences). The lad who was assaulted was waiting to speak to me and Ste. We both thanked him for what he had done and said we would see him for a drink when we got out. I haven't seen the lad for a long time but I wish him well.

Back in Hindley we had some laughs, especially two lads a couple of cells away. I know it sounds bad, saying that I was having a laugh in prison but that is the truth. I did have a laugh. The last time I was in Hindley a few months prior it was a living nightmare, but being in there with your best mate, along with a few good lads who have your back, makes things a lot easier.

Saying that, Hindley was still a shit hole. There was a hell of a lot of bullying going on in there. It was relentless with the constant noise echoing around the wing. That meant that you couldn't help but get caught up in it all. You could hear the relentless banging and the shouting for some poor kid to get to his window and give the baying crowd a chorus of Ten Cheesy Bell Ends. The banging and shouting would intensify until the kid started singing and they would then continue onto the next poor soul, where the ritual would be repeated. The good thing about being in our circle was that we were never bothered by anyone, I felt sorry for the vulnerable people in there. It's a dog eat dog world and you have to survive the best you can.

The weekends were long in Hindley because we were banged up twenty-three hours a day, unless you were on a visit, which broke the days up. Someone would be banging the tunes out of their window. 1991 was a great year for music and we would all be singing along to Crystal Waters' 'Gypsy Women', with everyone singing ladadee ladddar. My mum and nanna Naden used to come and see me but I them coming to see me in prison. I will always be grateful, even though at the time I too selfish to consider their feelings. As long as I got my parcel order and a visit, I was happy.

One Sunday, Earlsey was expecting a visit so he was really excited, putting on his best gear so he could look nice. I wasn't expecting one so I was just chilling on my bed. As the time of the visits was coming up, he was pacing the cell and every time he heard the rattle of the screws' keys, he would stand next to the door it to open, as people started getting called out for their visits. I could see that Ste was getting more and more anxious because he couldn't understand what was going on. Finally, half an hour later a screw finally unlocked the door and Earlsey was up like a whippet. He said he'd see me in a bit and that's when the screw said the visit is for Costello. Ste's face said it all as I left him in the cell and I went on my visit. I wasn't expecting a visit that day but I was happy to see my mum, and brothers. When time was up, I was returned to my cell and found Ste who couldn't believe that he had been let down. To be honest, I felt for him as there was nothing worse than spending all your time looking forward to a visit only for it does not happen. He just lay on the top bunk in silence and wouldn't even talk to me, he was that pissed off. After about an hour of trying to talk to him, I gave up then I thought 'fuck it'. I was bored and I thought I would wind him up. I asked if he'd had a visit today and kept teasing him. This continued for about half an hour with Ste getting more and more pissed off. It got to the point where he warned me that if I said it one more time he was going to jump down off the bunk and smack me. So, being a good mate, I did it again and he flew off the top bunk and punched me straight in the face, like he said he would. I jumped up and punched him back and before you knew it, we were having a free-for-all in the cell. I grabbed the empty water jug he said, 'come on then!' pointing to his head.

At this point there was a standoff between us, as we stared at each other, me holding a water jug, you could hear all the other people at their windows shouting that we were off our heads for fighting with each other. We both continued looking at each other until we started smiling then started laughing. I put the jug down and we put our arms around each other and had a hug. I said I was sorry for taking the piss and that was the end of that, as we looked around, we had wrecked our pad. We had a bench where we put all our letters and toiletries but they were everywhere. As we started tiding our cell up all you could hear was everyone shouting. Visits are important just like letters are when you are in prison. When you are expecting one and you don't get it then it really can affect you.

I was taken back to Macclesfield magistrates court to be sentenced for stealing the stereos and being carried in a stolen car. I had pleaded guilty to these offences at the first opportunity and was given three points on my driving licence…even though I didn't have a driving licence. I was given a fine for stealing the car stereos and then committed to Chester Crown court for trial for the assault on the lad that had been saying stuff about my family. I was also facing the affray charge that was due for trial as well. I was remanded back to Hindley and it wasn't long before me and Earlsey were told we were being shipped out to Stoke Heath in Shropshire.

I had heard stories about the place being violent and rife with bullying but that just about sums up every young offender institution in the country. Like I have said you had to be strong to survive. I'm sure it is still the same up and down the country today, in 2020.

I arrived at Stoke Heath in the summer of 1991 with court cases pending and two guilty verdicts. I was looking at a couple of years in jail so I wasn't looking at going home any time soon. I got placed on B wing in a single cell and Earlsey was next door. I was told to make my bed up and then banged up for the rest of the day.

After a couple of days, I was allocated to the Education wing and Earlsey was there as well. When we walked into the classroom, I saw Rick, who was from Macclesfield. I hadn't seen him for a while as he had been in jail for a couple of years so it was good to see him and we had a laugh in the classroom. They call it 'being on education' but the reality was that you just sat in the classroom doing extraordinarily little in the way of learning. Let's be honest, what young offender is going to learn anything other than how to burgle someone's home in these establishments?

On B wing, our pads overlooked a big field where there was a farmer driving a tractor going about his business. Earlsey used to shout out of the window "Oh Cozzy, look quick!" so I would go to my window he'd add "Look, your dad's coming to visit you!" and everyone would start laughing.

One-time Earlsey went too far with regards to shouting out of the window. Our cells overlooked the pathway, where the screws used to walk when they were arriving on the wing to start their shifts. One day some lad underneath me was screaming that he was going to do a screw in and waving some kind of homemade shank out of the window. This went on for about an hour until the mufti squad stormed his cell and dragged him down the block.

One night the screws were leaving and as they started walking up the path, Earlsey shouted out of the window that his name was Marc Costello I am in cell 326 and I don't give a fuck. It started off as funny until he carried it on for a few more nights, and everyone was laughing. The following morning, I told him that he needed to stop it and he said he would. That night I was lying on my bed when it started again, with everyone laughing. I ignored it and fell asleep.

During the night I was sound asleep when my cell door flew open and about six screws, all in riot gear came storming in. I was dragged out of bed and pinned up against the wall, where they started shouting at me, asking who did I think I was threatening the screws. I proper shit myself as you can imagine and was given a warning and thrown back on the bed as they walked out.

I didn't sleep well after that. Earlsey came to my cell in the morning. He heard what had gone on and we both started laughing our heads off. He stopped doing it after that but I suppose we were even after me winding him up over his no visit.

The bullying was unbelievable in Stoke Heath. There was a lad in there who, looking back, obviously had mental health problems, but at that time that was never even thought of. We called him John a Berry. I don't know if that was his name or where he came from, all I know was he was scruffy and he stank with really bad body odour. His hair was all over the place and you could see that he shouldn't have even been in prison, he would have been more suited to a hospital. Everyone in there was ripping into him and I mean it was relentless. They took all his burn off him, then made him smoke tea bags.

One day at dinner time, me and Earlsey got our food and sat with him at a table. After I had finished, I stood up to take my tray to the wash area, when I got told to sit down, I did this looking confused, where I got told that John a Berry cleared the table. Another time I was on association with Ste, watching telly, where a group of lads had hold of John a Berry and they were ordering him to fight another lad. He obviously wanted no part in it but unfortunately didn't have much choice in the matter. A couple of lads kept a lookout for the screws, then everyone watched as they started fighting. In a perverse sort of way, even though I knew it was wrong, you couldn't help but watch what was unfolding before your eyes. It was like a car crash but God it was funny watching these two fight each other. I think they even got a bit of respect from their tormenters for actually going ahead with it.

The screws finally came in and broke it up and John a Berry was led away feeling grateful it was all over. He was never seen again on that wing and I wonder what life has offered that poor soul in the last thirty year. Who knows?

My time was coming to an end in Stoke Heath. Me and Earlsey were being transferred back to Hindley so we could attend court. Ste had a few outstanding charges as well as the affray we were both charged with. I also had the assault that was due to be sent to the Crown court and I was getting fed up now with all this hanging over me. I just wanted to get it sorted out, come what may.

Chapter 14 – A Pair of Trainers and a Game of Pool and a Cream Bun

I arrived back in Hindley and found that I had been placed on a different wing from Earlsey. After a couple of days, I was allocated a job in the kitchens which meant that I would have more time out of my cell. I soon settled into the long days in there. Time was flying as I waited for my trial date. Things weren't all plain sailing in the though. There was a lad working in the kitchens who was a scouser and who was always giving it the big one; loudmouth and a bully with it. He would always pick on a couple of lads, getting them to do his jobs, taking bits of food off them, just being an absolute dick. He used to wear these smart Reebok classics that he was always going on about.

One day we were cleaning the kitchen area when, as usual, this scouser was sat about ordering these lads around like they were his lackeys. I had had enough and shouted at him to stop lazing around and help out. He asked me who did I think I was talking to and at that point a screw in. I just stared at the scouser who was now doing his bit to help out but I was pissed off with his attitude and sick of him bullying these lads every time a screw's back was turned. I knew that if we came to blows, he wouldn't have lasted long with me, so I wasn't bothered about him and his loudmouth.

A couple of days later he was hosing down the kitchen and because it was wet, he had taken off his Reeboks and was wearing wellington boots. I had a brain wave and thought let's give him a taste of his own medicine. So, I went into the changing area and looked in a couple of lockers until I came across his pride and joy, the Reebok classics. After checking no one was looking, I grabbed the trainers and bundled them up in my jumper and walked out. I wasn't that sure what I was going to do with them. I was thinking of hiding them for a while to wind him up then return them but that was until I heard his big mouth, bellowing across the kitchen at some poor lad. I thought "right, say goodbye to your trainers pal" and placed them inside the waste bin and buried them under all the leftover food. The bin was due to get emptied soon so I continued doing my jobs, laughing to myself.

About an hour passed and the scouser had finished and had put everything away and had gone into the changing. It wasn't long before he came out ranting and raving, asking if anyone had seen his trainers. Obviously, no one said anything because I hadn't told anyone what I'd done. He was accusing everyone; asking for them to be returned and this bully was almost in tears when everyone said they didn't know what he was on about. I looked over at the two lads who had been bullied by this guy and winked. They knew then that I was behind it but they wouldn't say anything.

What happened next amazed me though. This so-called bully, who had been giving it the big one, only went and reported his trainers missing to a screw. I couldn't believe it. There is one thing in jail that you don't do and that's go grassing to the screws. Everyone in the kitchen was told to line up whilst the screws asked us if anyone knew anything. We all said that we hadn't seen them and the screws then ordered the kitchen to be locked down whilst they did a full search. We were told to get changed and go back to our cells until they had finished the search. I started to feel a bit bad about everyone getting banged up but I wasn't arsed about the scouser because he deserved all he got. So, I went up to a screw and told him and he asked me to show him where I had put the trainers but it was too late. The bin had been emptied by an outside contractor so they had gone forever.

I was told to get changed as I was being taken back to my cell, everyone else was told to put their whites back on and get back to work. Back on my wing I was banged up and sacked from the kitchen. This meant I was now on twenty-three hour bang up.

The following morning after breakfast a screw opened my cell door and told me to get my stuff packed as I was moving cells. The cell I was in was the twos, for the kitchen, servery and cleaners and I was being moved on to the threes. I was also handed a piece of paper by the screw which said I was being nicked for theft of the trainers. I would be appearing in front of the governor the following morning.

Next day I was taken down the block and placed in the punishment cells whilst I waited to be called in front of the governor. For the next hour or so I could hear cells opening and then shutting as people were taken to the adjudication room. Soon it was my turn and I was led in. The charge was read out and I was asked if I pleaded guilty or not guilty. I said I was guilty and the screw read out the facts. The governor asked if I had anything to say, which I didn't and he then said because I was on remand and I had no remission to lose, I was sentenced to three days solitary confinement, which meant I was to stay in the punishment block. Unfortunately for me this was on a weekend so I would be there until Monday. I was due a visit on the Sunday; my mum was coming to see me with our Danny, but I had lost that privilege. I asked the screws if I could make a phone call but that was refused. I told them about my visit but they weren't bothered about that either. I was on punishment and that was it.

When I finally spoke to my mum she was fuming. She told me that she had travelled all that way with Danny in tow, had queued up with all the other visitors, only to be told by a screw that there was no visit because I was in the punishment block. She was told this in front of the other visitors, so she was upset and embarrassed by my actions. I was in prison yet I couldn't behave in there. The weekend dragged, sat in a cell for twenty-four hours a day with nothing except the four walls to look. I was glad to get back on the wing.

When I got back in my cell, I had received a letter from my solicitor telling me that I was due to attend magistrates court for a two-day trial with Earlsey, and the two lads we were fighting with, for affray. The trial was the following week.

That night I was lying on my bed when I heard someone shout out of the windows, 'oh Macclesfield sing us a song'. I thought 'who the fuck is this?' then I heard it again. I got up and I could see that this was happening on A wing which was facing my side across the yard. He started singing and I realised it was Scott. "Jesus!" I thought, "What is going on?" Scott was padded up with Ste Day.

Scott being Scott wouldn't shut up. He was singing away like they wanted him to and everyone was screaming at him to shut up. I was laughing my head off at him, typical Scott, he didn't care. It wasn't long before he got smacked off someone. Scott and Ste got moved over to B wing and they were in the cell above mine. We would spend hours talking out the window, having a laugh just passing the time.

The night before I was due for trial, I had a brand-new prison jumper and I wanted to give it to Ste Day so when I went down for tea, I asked a screw but he said no. Later, I had an idea and shouted to Ste to send me a line down. I had a hole in the mesh on my cell window, which was big enough with a bit of time and effort to get the jumper up. Eight hours later and we finally got the job done. I told Earlsey what had gone on the following morning as we waited to get escorted to court and he hadn't known they were in either.

When we arrived at court everyone was wondering where to put me and Earlsey. The problem was, as we got told, keeping us apart from the lad who was our co-accused. He was also the lad who had stabbed me and he was coming from Walton Prison in Liverpool where he was doing four years. I wasn't bothered about seeing him but we were placed in the cages at the back of the court, whilst he was brought in and placed in a room with his solicitor. Our solicitor came to see us with some news. Our co-accused had asked to see me and Earlsey because he wanted to do a deal with us.

We were all placed in a room with our briefs, we shook hands and everything was fine. What he wanted us all to do was to agree to all plead guilty because with him doing four years for stabbing me he would get a concurrent sentence instead of any more time but that would have meant me and Earlsey getting a custodial which we were guaranteed anyway with a guilty verdict. On the slim hope of getting a not guilty, we would not get any jail time so we said we would think about it and went to talk with our solicitor. I could see what he was saying and with the evidence stacked against us, it was highly unlikely that we would get found not guilty. So, we agreed to plead guilty to the charge of affray.

After our solicitors had spoken on our behalf we were sentenced. Me and Earlsey got four months.

Our co-accused got six months concurrent, and his mate got six months. We were then taken back into the holding area where our co-accused thanked us as he was taken back to Walton with his mate. I thought that me and Ste would be going back to Hindley but instead we were going to Wetherby in Yorkshire. I had never heard of the place neither had Earlsey. Wetherby was a former naval base called HMS Ceres and it got changed to a borstal in 1958. It then became a young offenders institution so we made the journey not knowing what to expect. When we arrived, we went straight to the reception where we were processed and placed on to the induction wing for the night. The following morning, we were taken to the stores where we got allocated our kit and then carried it over to the house block where we would be placed. We were placed in single cells and told to make our beds up.

There were two house blocks at the time in Wetherby, both with semi-open conditions and an induction wing near the reception that acted as a punishment wing as well. When I went down for dinner, I was surprised to see a couple of lads that I knew from Macclesfield in there, Justin and Gez. Soon we were all knocking about together and having a laugh and one night on association I was watching Justin and Gez playing pool. Ste had been on the phone and came over and asked who was next on. Justin said no one, so Ste said he would play the winner. Just then, a lad walked over and announced that he was next and when Ste argued he told him to fuck off. I just looked at Ste and was thinking 'here we go' as Ste told the lad to get outside the unit.

Now, this is how mad life inside a young offenders' can be. Fighting over absolutely nothing, madness really especially as two men was going to have a fight over who was next on the pool table. Anyway, they both went outside and I was thinking they would be back in a couple of minutes with everything forgotten. Five minutes passed and I decided to go outside to see what was happening but as I started walking towards the door the other guy came walking in. His face was a mess with blood all over it and there was a hole in his cheek. Ste then walked in looking as bad as the lad. His face was bloody and he showed me his ear…which was hanging off. I asked him if he'd won and he laughed and said no. The screws came over and saw that they'd been fighting and nicked them both but then spotted Ste's ear and started shouting for the medical screw. He was sat on a chair with a towel against his head to stem the blood.

The medical screw took one look and said that he needed to go to the outside hospital to have it stitched back on. The other lad would also be going to the hospital to have his cheek looked at. This was serious because, obviously, Ste was a prisoner and would have to be granted permission to be allowed to go to the hospital. All this over who was next on at pool, you couldn't make it up.

Earlsey then told me what had happened outside. They had started fighting and when they were on the floor the lad had bit Ste's ear and wouldn't let go so Ste decided to get his own back and sunk his teeth into the lad's cheek and wouldn't let go. I didn't see him until the following morning when he came back on the unit to get his belongings, as he was being taken to the punishment block.

I had been in Wetherby now for about three weeks when I got talking to a lad from Manchester. He was asking me how long I had been in for, the usual shit, so I told him that I had been in for a few months on remand, first in Hindley and Stoke Heath, then here for a few weeks doing my sentence. He started talking about remission and time on remand and explained that the time I had spent in jail on remand could be taken off the time that I had served, meaning that I could go home sooner. I told him that I was in for Affray but I didn't know if I had done any remand for that charge. Even though I had done about four months on remand I had gone to court for all different charges. The lad told me to go and see the screws and tell them that I wanted to apply for my remand back. This was just after breakfast, so I went up to the screws' office and asked. I was given a form and told to fill it out with the dates that I had been on remand and which prison I had been in at the times. I quickly filled it out and handed it back. I didn't think much more of it and went to work as normal with everyone else.

After dinner we were back at work, when a screw came over to me and said I was wanted back on the unit. I walked straight up to the screws' office and had asked me my name and number. He then said he had some good news for me as he handed me a fax confirming that I was being released immediately. I had got all my remand days back; I was going home.

I couldn't believe it; I ran up to my cell and grabbed all my personal belongings. I was buzzing and soon word had got round and a few lads came to my cell to see me. I gave them my toiletries and any credit that was left on my phonecards and then went back to the screws' office and asked if Ste was coming home too but they didn't know.

I started walking towards the reception when I cut across to where Earlsey's cell was. I knocked on his window and told him about the time on remand counting against this sentence. As you can imagine, Ste was going mad. I left Ste as he was pressing his buzzer, banging on his cell door and shouting for the screws to let him go home. At reception he was trying to explain that he had been in jail the same time as me for the same offense and the screw told him that they would look into it for him. I handed my stuff in and was given a box with my clothes in. As I started getting changed, I looked to my right and Earlsey was taking his clothes off as well. I started laughing as the screw was shouting to Earlsey to put his prison clothes back on, and Earlsey was refusing, saying he was going with me. It was like watching a Laurel and Hardy sketch or the Chuckle Brothers. In the end the screws told Earlsey to sit down whilst they made some enquiries. Ste had given them the dates he had been on remand and it didn't take long for them to come back with the good news that he was going home as well.

We were both released that windy autumn afternoon in October 1991 and given a discharge grant and a travel warrant back to Macclesfield. We got a lift to Wetherby town centre from a screw driving a minibus but then had to catch a bus to Leeds, then a train to Manchester and then another train home. As we were walking towards the bus station, we passed a bakery where, in the window, there was a tray of cream cakes, Ste announced that he really fancied a cream cake and after he bought it he pulled the greaseproof paper off that was covered in cream and dropped it on the floor but the wind caught it. There was an old lady with a walking stick about ten yards behind us and unfortunately the wind carried the paper through the air and hit the old lady in the face. I have to apologise for laughing but I have never seen anything as funny. It was one in a million and no harm was done.

When we got back in Macclesfield, we parted company and headed our separate ways home. I hadn't told any of my family that I was released, in my mind I wanted to surprise them. I don't know what I was thinking really, as they had been glad that I wasn't there causing a bad atmosphere with my selfish antics and they were happy without the drama that I brought home every time I went out. When I walked through the door the reception was lukewarm. On one hand they were happy that I was out of prison as I had been away from home for about five months but on the other hand, they were obvious thinking about how long would it be before I started bringing my shit to their door again. It turned out that my stay at home was short as I was due at Chester Crown court for the assault charge in ten days. I had every intention of going not guilty on this charge, my defence was that I had acted in self-defence due to the lad slagging my family off and I was defending my family name. Unfortunately, the fact that I had gone over the top on the lad as usual due to being full of alcohol, it meant that self-defence was not a defence that I could use. I had followed the lad and given him a beating even though he had admitted calling my family names. I would have to plead guilty and face the consequences.

I stood in the dock at Chester Crown court and pleaded guilty to section forty-seven assault. My barrister stood up and outlined the facts: That I was provoked; that I was sorry and all the usual stuff to make you look good in the eyes of the court. The problem was I had only been out of prison for ten days and my criminal record was horrific especially for violence and especially when I had been drinking. In just under eighteen months I had gone from having no criminal record to standing in court looking at a possible further spell inside. The judge retired to consider his sentence and I had already been warned it was looking like I would go down and it would depend just on how long. When the judge returned, I was sentenced to twelve months in prison. I had been out of Wetherby for just ten days.

I was taken from Chester Crown back to Hindley to start my new sentence. As I lay in my cell that night, I remember feeling happy and relieved that all this was over, I could see a light at the end of the tunnel. Yes, I was in jail and yes, I was doing a twelve-month sentence and yes, I would be in jail for Christmas and my birthday BUT it felt like a massive weight had been lifted from my shoulders. During 1991 I had spent most of the year either on bail or in jail except for those ten days that I was briefly home for. I had to sort myself out and break this cycle that I was in before it was too late.

I was only in Hindley for a couple of weeks before I was moved to Stoke Heath. I had only been in Stoke Heath for a week or so before I was moved back to Wetherby. November 24th, 1991. I remember the date because I was in the reception at Stoke Heath waiting for the escort to take me to Wetherby, when it was announced that Freddie Mercury had died. He had released a statement a day or so before saying that he had aids but even so it was a shock and everyone was talking about it.

I arrived back at Wetherby where I knew a few familiar faces. It was a good job I had been generous giving my stuff away when I was told I was going home, otherwise that could have caused me a few problems when I got back.

I hadn't been back long when I got into a fight with some lad. I can't remember where he was from but he was big. I had clocked him a couple of times, trying to bully a couple of guys and one day I was in the dining hall and had just started to eat when someone appeared, demanding that I move out of his seat. I turned and looked and it was the lad who had been throwing his weight around. I knew I had two options. I could either say nothing and move tables and get known as an easy touch or I could tell him to fuck off and that I was not moving. I decided to tell him to fuck off and carried on eating my dinner. He walked off and got another seat a nearby table and sat there trying to intimidate me by staring at me. I just stared back until one of us blinked first. It was quite amusing to be fair but, like I said, you have to show no sign of weakness otherwise everyone will jump all over you. That's why Earlsey went outside with that lad and that's why I told this lad to fuck off. You have got to stand up for yourself no matter what, survival of the fittest.

After a day of this lad trying to intimidate me, I decided I had had enough, I was going to confront him and get it over with. That night we were on association and I was watching television with a couple of blokes when we decided to go to the gym. On the way there I saw the lad walking towards us, so I stopped and asked him what his problem was. He didn't look that keen as I don't think he had expected me to offer him out, but he couldn't back down in front of others. As he walked towards me, I smacked him in the head and he went backwards and I was on him. I gave him a couple of digs and when one of the lads shouted the screws was coming, we stopped fighting and I walked off towards the gym with the others. Everyone started talking about what had happened and I was seen as someone who wouldn't take any shit, so that made life easier.

I saw the lad the following morning at breakfast but he didn't say anything and a few days later we sorted things out and he turned out not to be a bad lad to be fair. That's prison life for you, fighting over nothing.

When I was in Wetherby I was given the job as number one in the stores. This meant I was in charge of issuing the kit out on kit change day and also giving the packs out to all new arrivals who came into the reception. I had a good number going on in the stores. I used to get stamps and phonecards off the lads in exchange for a descent shirt or an extra pair of boxers and socks. The time was flying in there. I was getting fitter by going to the gym and eating healthily, so things were looking up. I was getting on well with my parents, which was a good thing too and I had a visit one day from my uncle Jimmy who had brought my mum and brothers up to see me.

I was surprised that Jimmy had come all that way until he explained that on their way back home, they were going to visit Peter Sutcliffe the Yorkshire Ripper's home in Bradford. Our Jimmy was obsessed with anything like that so he wouldn't have missed out on a chance to see the Ripper's house even if it meant visiting me first.

I spent Christmas and New Year 1991 in jail. I thought it would be bad in prison for Christmas but I imagine it is worse for the families on the outside who are missing their loved ones. When you are in prison, Christmas Day is just like a Sunday except you get a bit of Christmas dinner and an hour extra association. New Year's Eve I was asleep early so I slept through to the following morning.

I was due to be released in February 1992 and a month before my release day I was allowed out on a town visit in Wetherby. This is where you are allowed to spend a few hours out of the prison with your family and you can walk around, have some dinner, and enjoy time with your loved ones before your release. My mum and dad and brothers all came up and we had a good time seeing what the town had to offer. It was good spending time as a family and I really hoped that things would be different when I was released the following month. I didn't deserve the love my family had shown me. They had all stood by me when I didn't give a shit about anyone but myself.

I walked out of Wetherby Young Offender institute on 13th February 1992 vowing never to return.

Chapter 15 – Sheep Dogs to Crown Court Trials

On my release I returned to the family home and obviously my family were skeptical.

They had been in this position before, listening to me promise that I was going to change my ways, and that I was putting all this shit behind me, I really wanted to be the son that they all could be proud of. I had every intention of keeping my word and that this was going to be a new start. However, my problem has always been alcohol and at that time in my life I just couldn't control what I was doing when I was drinking. I wouldn't listen to anyone and my reputation around Macclesfield fueled the madness that drink had brought on. Nowadays people would say what I did was binge drinking. I would go out and get pissed out of my mind on anything that was put in front of me, then I would start acting up to my reputation. That meant no one was safe and if someone looked at me funny or if I heard someone had been saying shit about me then they were having it. I just couldn't let things go and I was dangerous and nasty yet I thought, in my tiny mind, that I was king of the kings.

Things did start to settle down and one day I walked into our house when my dad said that he had got me a job working with him on the scaffolding. The following Monday I started and began getting close to my dad, through working with him. He was a hard-working, well respected man in the scaffolding business and I enjoyed seeing a different side to him, away from home.

When I finished work on a Friday, I had started going up Daz's house for a drink before we went into town. We would buy a bottle of vodka and drink it at his house between us, then go into town. This started becoming a Friday ritual that we did for a few months. I was working, earning good money and I should have been saving and thinking about my future. I was 19 years old with the rest of my life ahead of me, yet I was pissing it all up against the wall. I was drinking a lot more now that I could afford it and I had started seeing Babs, a girl whose brother I was knocking about with from the flats. I was with Babs for the next 16 years on and off and we got married but it didn't work out and we divorced in 2003. We have two kids: Gabriella and Connell.

I had been seeing Babs for a few weeks when I decided to go and have a few pints one Saturday afternoon. A few hours later I ended up in the Mulberry Bush pub on the estate where I lived. I was pissed out of my head, when the landlord decided that he wasn't going to serve me anymore. Well, I went up like a bottle of pop and started trying to get hold of the landlord before, thankfully, a load of the regulars grabbed hold of me and threw me out of the door.

I staggered off home only to find that Babs had been sat in my bedroom waiting for me for the last few hours. Obviously, my parents weren't impressed with the state that I was in, so a row started between that resulted in the straw breaking the camel's back. I was totally out of order with what I said and I didn't mean it but, like my mum said, I never did mean it. The line was crossed and I never lived with my family again. I walked out of the house and went and stayed at Babs's mum's house in the flats.

Not long after moving in with Babs's mum, my uncle Frank got sent to prison so we moved into his flat to look after it for him while he was away. That gave me time to get on the housing list, where I was soon offered my own place.

In 1994 my daughter Leigh Gabriella was born. Gaby was always known by her middle name as it is a tradition on Babs's side and that's what we decided to continue. Gaby was born just before I turned twenty-one and this should have been the turning point in my life. For a time, I did settle down and things were looking good. I was working, I was a dad now, I had responsibilities, and most of all I had a beautiful baby girl that I loved. You would have thought I would stay in and embrace my family life. At first, I did and my intentions were good. I started having the odd Friday night out with my mates but this started leading into my going out on Saturdays which then became my day out. I worked all week, staying in with my family, then Saturday I was out on the piss all day with my mates and after a while this led to going out Sundays after football. This obviously didn't go down well at home and it caused a lot of arguments which resulted in me staying out on the piss instead of being with my daughter.

My selfish behaviour was my downfall, and during this time I started taking whizz and then ecstasy as well as drinking. This meant that I would be going out on a Saturday morning, then staying out all night, ending up at someone's house or flat talking shit and thinking that I was having a brilliant time. In the meantime, Babs would be sat at home with Gaby wondering where I was. This would continue in the same vein every weekend but in my eyes, I was doing nothing wrong, I was working, paying my way. Saturday was my time and I would do whatever I wanted. The only difference was that I wasn't getting into trouble with the police.

I was still getting into fights around town though. With the influx of ecstasy around Macclesfield, everyone was dropping pills and would rather have a cuddle instead of a fight so any bad blood was soon forgotten when we were all out of our heads. The next time I got arrested was for criminal damage. We used to go up to Daz's house where his dad Brian used to make homebrew. He had gallons of the stuff and Brian was famous for it. Everyone was more than welcome to call up and have a few pints and one Sunday I was with Babs and her brother when we called in to see Daz. He wasn't there but Brian invited us in to wait for him and, after a few minutes, asked us if we wanted to sample a couple of pints of homebrew. As you can imagine, a couple of hours later we were staggering back down the road. We got a taxi up to the Wharf pub near the town centre and I got into an argument with Babs so I stormed off out onto the street. I then jumped on to the first parked car that I came across and started trying to kick the windscreen in. Then I punched the driver's window until it smashed, opened the door and let the handbrake off. I then pushed the car so that it ran into the car that was in front. I then did the same to the next car while everyone was out of the pub wondering what was going on. The owners of the cars were all in the street looking at the damage that I had just caused. I was completely off my head at this point and I was arrested at the scene and charged with three counts of criminal damage. I couldn't remember a thing about it because I had blacked out.

When I appeared at Macclesfield magistrates court, I pleaded guilty straight away. My solicitor pointed out to me that this was a serious charge and with my criminal record I could be going to prison. I had been out of trouble for a couple of years but that wouldn't count for a lot. The case was adjourned for reports with the probation recommending community service but I was expecting a spell behind bars. When I went back for sentencing, I got community service but the magistrate made it clear that this was my final chance. The fact that I had a young daughter and I had kept my nose clean had made a difference but this was it for me, no more chances. I was in the following edition of the Macclesfield Express with the headline 'Young Dad Gets His Final Warning'. I thanked the magistrate and decided that I wouldn't be back before him again. Unfortunately, my good intentions didn't last long.

What happened at the Macclesfield sheep dog trials wasn't down to me but I was involved along with my brother Terry and a lad named Stuart. The sheep dog trials are an annual event that take place in Sutton, a little village just outside Macclesfield. In the day, the farmers hold competitions and at night there is a big marquee set up in a field where there is a bar and a disco. I had been drinking in town when a few of us, including Terry and Stuart, decided to go up there. I don't know why we ended up there as I had never before and I haven't since. When we got there the night was in full swing so we got a drink and walked around seeing if we knew anyone. The thing with these events is they are full of the farming community; you are in their world so you tend to stick out like a sore thumb. The atmosphere was good, I was enjoying the night and I ended up chatting to a couple of people when an argument started near to the disco. I looked over and saw that our Terry and Stuart were arguing with a couple of lads and the next thing I know is a fight broke out. I ran over and grabbed one of the lads and went to get him off our Terry. He swung for me so I punched him and after a minute the fight finished and we walked out and went home. I didn't think anything more about it.

About a month or so later one morning, there was a knock on the door and it was a CID who said he was arresting me for two section forty-seven assaults on a couple lads at the sheep dog trials. I couldn't believe it. I had forgotten all about that and I hadn't done much wrong, it was mainly Terry and Stuart who had been involved, not me in the way the police were accusing me of. The problem I faced was that I was the only one arrested in connection with what had gone on. Our Terry wasn't and neither was Stuart. I was never going to drop them in it as well because I am not a grass so it was just me in the frame.

After speaking with my solicitor, it was decided that I would go 'no comment' when I was interviewed and afterwards, I was asked if I would attend an identity parade. I said I would, so I was bailed until the following week.

This was an absolute farce. There were twelve of us all stood in a line. None of us even looked the same and it was like a sketch show. My solicitor complained and we swapped a couple of people before I took my place in the line-up. I was picked out by one of them but not the other one and this caused the police a bit of a problem because there was no real evidence against me. I had gone 'no comment' and now I had only been picked out of the parade by one of them but in their statements, they were adamant it was definitely me that had assaulted them both.

Ruth spoke to the police to see what was going on and I was # bailed for a couple of weeks while the police decided what was happening. I went to see Stuart to ask him to help me as he had been the one that had been involved in the fight but Stuart unfortunately didn't see it that way. As far as he was concerned, he was out of it and he was staying that way. I couldn't believe what he was saying. Stuart was involved more than I was and had been from the initial argument that I wasn't involved in. He had kicked off with the lads along with our Terry, but I wasn't the only one guilty of assaulting two lads that night. I asked Stuart for help and he refused saying that he couldn't afford to get arrested and convicted for assault as he was doing a college course, or something, and couldn't afford to throw that away. This caused a lot of bad blood between us that resulted in me trying to attack him every time I saw him. Looking back now I can understand what he was saying. Yes, we were all involved and it could have been any one of us that got pulled in but unfortunately with my reputation it was me who was the one they came for.

I haven't seen Stuart since those days. With all the shit I was giving him, Stuart took the opportunity to move out of Macclesfield and start a new life in Stoke-on-Trent. I sent him a message when I started writing this book where I apologised for my actions. I was in the wrong for trying to put pressure on him and I was more in the wrong to threaten him every time I saw him and for assaulting him. I can only apologise and I wish him well.

Our Terry was involved as well but he had just started a job as an apprentice electrician and he couldn't let a fight jeopardise his future, that's why he was kept out of it. Terry came to my trial and was going to stand up and tell the court that it was him not me that assaulted the guys which I thanked him for but it was pointed out to Terry that if he did this they could charge him with the assaults at a later date so it was agreed he wouldn't give evidence for me. I thank him for trying though.

I was charged with two section forty-seven assaults and committed to Chester Crown court for trial on Tuesday 14th March 1995.

From the start of the trial I knew I was in trouble. The judge had taken an instant dislike to me, that much was obvious. When the prosecution started outlining their case, I could see the judge looking at me with disgust on his face. The case boiled down to my word against the two complainants. There were no other witnesses called and my defence centred on me being an innocent bystander who was watching a fight between my brother Terry, Stuart, and the complainants. The prosecution's case was that me and others had assaulted the two guys, so it was pretty straight forward who would the jury believe. The first complainant gave evidence and said that he was enjoying a night out when all of a sudden, he had been assaulted by a couple of lads. He said at first, he didn't know who it was but then he recognised me. He was asked was he sure that it was me and he said yes, he had seen me walking around the Hurdsfield estate on a few occasions. Given that, and the fact that he had picked me out on the ID parade, he looked like a solid witness at face value.

My barrister cross-examined him and after a few questions on how sure he was that it was me who was involved, it turned out that his girlfriend lived around the corner from my mum and dad and had told him that it was me when they'd both seen me walking around the estate. So, his evidence didn't look quite so good now. The prosecution then called the other guy who had also been assaulted and his evidence was sketchy to say the least. He said that he was fighting with a couple of lads but couldn't be sure if one of them was me. He also hadn't picked me out of the ID parade.

I then went into the dock and, as agreed, I put all the blame on our Terry and Stuart. It had been them who were fighting and the witness had got me mixed up with our Terry as he was the one who lived on the estate not me. Then the prosecution, during cross-examination, tried to get me to admit that I was involved. I held firm and repeated that I hadn't and it was nothing to do with me. What I did say though, in my cross examination was 'when they were fighting'. This was important because when the judge summed up to the jury, he stated that I had said 'when we were fighting', which was misleading.

After all the summing up the jury retired to consider their verdict and after a couple of hours the case was adjourned with no decision. We all returned the following morning and my dad was there with Babs. We drank coffee whilst we awaited the jury's verdict and after a few hours we were called back into the court. I stood in the dock and scanned the faces of the jury, seeing if I could see which way this was going to go but I couldn't read them. The judge asked the foreman of the jury if they had all agreed on their verdict and the foreman said they had. On the first count of Assault Occasioning Actual Bodily Harm, the foreman said guilty. On the second count of Assault Occasioning Actual Bodily Harm, the foreman said guilty. I had been found guilty of both assaults and was surprised seeing that the evidence against me hadn't been conclusive. It had been stated in court by everyone that there were two people fighting with them yet I was the only one on trial.

My barrister stood up and asked the judge to adjourn sentencing pending reports by the probation service but the judge instantly dismissed this, stating that he didn't require any reports with regards to my sentencing. I knew then that I was going to prison, it was just for how long. My barrister started to speak on my behalf but he was dismissed. The judge had made up his mind. The prosecution read out my previous convictions to the court and it didn't make for good reading. I was expecting the worst and the judge then looked at me and proceeded to rip me to bits. He said I was a thug, I was violent, my record was appalling. I was thinking the worst and he then started sentencing me. On count one Assault Occasioning Actual Bodily Harm, twelve months in prison. On count two Assault Occasioning Actual Bodily Harm twelve months. I had also breached a conditional discharge for which I was sentenced to a further month in prison. The judge said the two, twelve months would be concurrent and the month would be consecutive meaning I was sentenced to a total of thirteen months in prison.

I was led down to the cells where I was processed and my barrister came down to see me. He brought my dad and Babs who were upset by what had happened. I told them not to worry and that I would be home before they knew it. My barrister said he was sorry and he was going to report the judge and his handling of the case because rom start to finish he was biased in favour of prosecution. It was too late now though because I was going to prison.

I said my goodbyes to dad and Babs and was placed in a cell at the court to await the outcome of the other case. You had to stay until the last case had finished so everyone who had been sent down could be transported to prison together. As I lay in my cell, thinking of what had just happened and especially with how the judge had been, if I am being honest, and even now looking back on this, I'm surprised that I only got twelve months concurrent for the assaults especially seeing that for my last sentence, I got twelve months as well. I thought this time I would be getting at least between two and three years, so thirteen months was a result. After the final case had finished, I was handcuffed and placed in a sweat box to make the journey to HMP Liverpool, also known as Walton.

Chapter 16 – Justice on The Strand

This was my first time in a proper prison. I had heard a few things about Walton but nothing good. A couple of years earlier me and my dad had visited my uncle Frank in there, I hadn't imagined that I would end up in there myself.

When we arrived at Walton, the driver was told to wait outside the prison as they were busy. We waited for what seemed like hours until they us in. The first thing I noticed was how busy the reception area was. It was like everyone and everything was going at 100 miles per hour. We were told to sit on a wooden bench until they called our names. When I walked forward to where a screw was sat behind a desk, he asked me questions like name, address, which court I had come from, what was the offence, and what sentence did I receive. I then handed in my property, which I signed for, and swapped my clothes for prison issue garments and got given a bed pack and was told to wait in a room until I was told which wing I would be placed on. I looked around to see if I knew anyone. It was full of lads, but I didn't know any of them.

I was taken to H wing and placed in a cell on the ground floor which absolutely stank of piss. There was a stale bucket in the corner of the room that did not have a lid on it. H wing was used for new arrivals and also inmates who had been allocated to other prisons. It was basic with piss pots still in some of the cells. The prison was being redeveloped in the wake of the Strangeways riots a few years ago, so toilets had been fitted on most of the wings, just not on H wing yet. I made my bed up then realised that I had no pillow, so I used my jumper. I fell asleep with my head under the green blanket trying to get away from the smell.

The following morning when we were unlocked to go to recess, I walked out and bumped straight into Scott Turnock. Scott had been sent down the day before as well but he was only doing a couple of weeks for non-payment of fines. I later found out that there were a few lads I knew from Macclesfield in Walton at the same time as me.

I was taken to see the allocation board a couple of days after I arrived, where they asked me where I wanted to serve my time. I requested Kirkham, an open prison but this was refused because I had violence on my record. I was told I would stay in Walton until I got allocated to another Cat C prison and then moved to a cell on another wing and this is where I started getting a few problems.

The fact is that Walton prison, back in 1995, was full of heroin and it was full of smackheads. I was padded up with a lad who was from Manchester and on first impressions he seemed alright, we chatted and got on. I was thinking that things weren't too bad but after a couple of days I realised he was a smackhead and this is where my problems started. I have never taken heroin and I never will yet here I was in prison with a guy who was doing it in front of me. He went into the toilet to do it, but it stank so he would then throw up in the toilet. I could never understand why anyone would take heroin. Yes, I have taken drugs but I would never cross that line. This lad would then just start cleaning the cell from top to bottom, whilst I lay on my bed watching him. He would then get into bed and go to sleep.

In Walton there is a big heating pipe that goes through all the cells on the wing. What people would do is, when they wanted to pass something to someone in another cell, get a page from a newspaper, fold it in half, then put whatever they were passing flat inside the paper. Then they would push it through to the next cell and so on, until it got to the right destination. This is how they got smack from one cell to the other without the screws finding out.

The lad I was padded up with was getting his smack from the lads next door, so he would be at the pipe most days, shouting through to the next cell. He would then be getting the parcels through the pipe, taking his bit out before passing it on to the next cell and hide it for later. He was loud and started to get obnoxious. I don't know if it was the smack he was taking or the fact he was trying to look hard with the lads next door who he was getting the smack off but he was pissing me off.

One day I was lying on my bed, when a parcel came through the pipe into the cell. After a minute or two there was a knock on the cell wall, followed by shouting. I got off my bed and saw that my pad mate was asleep. This was a problem because we had a parcel and someone else was waiting for it too. I certainly wasn't touching it. I just lay back on my bed and after a few minutes of shouting and banging my pad mate woke up, jumped of the top bunk and went to the pipe, saw the parcel and asked me how long it had been there. I said it about twenty minutes, and he began bawling at me, asking me why the fuck hadn't I woke him up or more importantly why hadn't I passed it on. I asked him who the fuck did he think he was talking to, he ignored me and proceeded to pass the parcel to the next cell so I stood up and again asked him who he was talking to. He said that I should have sorted the parcel out. I told him I was having nothing to do with it and he told me that the lads next door wouldn't like that.

This was where the problems started because we were on a twenty-three hour a day bang up in

Walton. This meant I was in this horrible environment, with drug dealers in the cell next door and with knobhead of pad mate. I was in hell so I just tried to ignore everyone. The days were long, especially with me being banged up all the time. Some days I would sleep for most of the day then all night, anything to make the days go faster.

During this time, I started getting a few threats from the dealers next door. I never really let it bother me. They were shouting that if I didn't pass the parcels down the pipe, they would see me on the yard and this amused me. I used to think that if they wanted me that badly I was only in the cell next door, my pad mate who was right up their arses, kept saying to me that I better do what they say or I would be getting it. I just told him to fuck off and leave me alone.

A couple of days later he asked me if I wanted a game of cards. I thought 'fuck it', I had nothing else to do so we started playing and after a while he began banging his hand on the table and with me being all relaxed it made me jump. He thought this was funny, so after a while he kept doing it. I told him to pack it in and he gave it the big one. When he did it again, I jumped off my chair and flew at him and started punching him in the head. We started grappling with each other and I was on top of him ready to fill him in. I asked if that was it and he just looked at me as I let him go. His nose was bleeding and he went into the toilet to clean himself up while I tided the cell up. When he came back, he got straight in bed. I didn't sleep at all that night and over the next couple of days things came to a head with him and the dealers next door.

He was saying shit to them about me, telling them I was still refusing to play ball and they would then start trying to intimidate me. I had been in this cell with my pad mate for about three weeks now and I was at my breaking point. One morning when my pad mate had gone out of the cell. I jumped off my bed and grabbed the table and smashed it on the floor and broke the chair leg off. I then put the table back, leaning it against the wall so it wouldn't fall over and put the chair leg under my pillow. When my pad mate returned, we were opened up for dinner and I let him go out first. I then grabbed the chair leg and walked straight into the cell next door where the drug dealers were.

I waved it at them both, asking if they wanted any trouble and if they did, we would sort it now. My head had gone and I was shaking with rage. This was ending now, one way or the other. they just looked at me and said that they didn't want any trouble. I told them that I wasn't into smack and I wasn't pushing their parcels for them, I just wanted to be left alone and they said they would forget it. I walked out and put the chair leg back the best I could. I think the dealers had a word with my pad mate because after that I didn't have any trouble off any of them.

I was soon moved from that wing and placed on to B wing where I landed a job as a wing cleaner. I only had this job a couple of weeks before I was sacked for talking to Earlsey at the wing gate. Ste was on a different wing to me and I hadn't seen him for a while. I was having a quick chat with him when a screw told me to get back to work. After dinner I was in my cell when a screw came in and told me to get my stuff as I was moving cells because I had been sacked for a security breach…having a chat with my mate.

I was then padded up with a lad from Toxteth. He was nice and chilled and we got on really well. He was in for drug dealing after being caught with a load of ecstasy tablets in his car. He was doing a couple of years and had been in Walton for a while so he had things boxed off. One Saturday he came back from a visit and he was smiling as he pulled his pants down and pulled a small bag out from his arse cheeks. It contained a load of ecstasy tablets. Later we listened to tunes all night as we each took an ecstasy tab and, for a few hours, it took me out of myself and out of the prison.

The following day out on the exercise yard I was walking around with Earlsey when we were joined by Gozzer who I went to school with. I hadn't seen Gozzer for a few years. He had been in and out of prison and it was good to see him again. I went to the gym with him once and never again. We did the circuit training until I was throwing up after Gozzer had put me through my paces.

I had been in Walton for about a month when I received a letter from my solicitor. She was telling me that after speaking to my barrister, they had decided that they had grounds to appeal against my conviction. This was unexpected but welcome news. It seemed that the judge in his summing up to the jury had misled them by informing them that I had said that "we" were fighting but what I had actually said was "they". My grounds for appeal were based on this wording and it seemed I had a chance of going home soon.

My solicitor came to see me and told me that they were going to lodge the appeal and it would first be heard before a judge who would then decide if there were enough grounds to send it to a higher court. A couple of weeks later this happened which was brilliant news. I just had to wait for a date to be listed but in the meantime, I had to sit tight and continue to serve my sentence.

One morning the cell door opened and a screw told me to get my belongings together, as I was moving to another prison. I asked him if this had anything to do with my appeal, but he said he did not know and just said I was on the list for transfers.

I collected all my belongings and said goodbye to my pad mate. In the reception area I found out I was going to HMP Shrewsbury. I wasn't sorry to see the back of Walton. I had spent two months in there and it's nothing but an absolute shithole. The move to Shrewsbury was a good one for me; a better prison and a hundred times better. It was clean and more relaxed than Walton. Shrewsbury had one big wing that housed all the inmates. I soon settled in with all my focus on the appeal. I was in contact with my solicitor, who kept me up to date with any developments. We were just waiting for the date to be listed and hopefully it would be sooner rather than later.

I had been in Shrewsbury for about a month when I got the news that my appeal would be heard in London at the end of July 1995, just over a month away. I was only glad to finally get a date so I could find out, one way or another. The last couple of months had been difficult with all the waiting and my solicitor had warned me it would be a slow process and she wasn't wrong. When it was finally heard, I would have served over four months of my sentence. If my appeal failed I would have about ten weeks left to serve. I had to remain positive but there was always some doubt that things might not work out the way you want

The court date set for my hearing was now ten days away and I was going to be produced at the hearing in London. I just presumed that I would travel down from Shrewsbury straight to the court but I was wrong on that score. I was told to get my belongings together because in the morning I was being moved back to Walton. My heart sank. I couldn't believe that I was going back to that shit hole.

That night I couldn't sleep. I was nervous, I was anxious about going back to Walton and, along with my appeal the following week, my mind was racing. It was a long night and it was daylight when I fell asleep only to be woken by the screws opening everyone up.

I had my breakfast before heading to the reception to wait for my transfer and was told that a couple of screws were coming down from Walton to collect to me. This I found strange, even more so when they turned up in a taxi. I was handcuffed to one of them and placed in the back seat. On the way the screws told me that I would only be in Walton for the weekend, because on Monday they would be taking me to a London prison and from there I would be taken to the Court of Appeal.

The weekend in Walton soon passed and Monday morning I was taken back to the reception where I was greeted by the same two screws that had collected me from Shrewsbury, with big smiles on their faces. I was handcuffed again and they told me they were getting overtime for escorting me and also a night out in London on expenses.

I was told that I would be going to HMP Brixton in South London and that this was the prison where everyone who was attending the appeal court was allocated. It was also a remand prison, as well as an allocation prison for sentenced inmates. The difference between Brixton and the northern prisons was huge, it was like being in a different world. For example, in Walton, as soon as you got there you sensed that it was an aggressive jail with everyone out for themselves. The atmosphere was toxic especially with the number of smackheads that were housed in there. Shrewsbury was more relaxed and everyone tried to get along with each other When I arrived in Brixton, I wasn't sure what to expect. I was a northerner in a London jail. I didn't have anything to worry about though, everyone was really friendly. People asked me if I needed anything and I was made to feel welcome. That was the difference between the prisons. In London, the inmates looked out for each other and that was a big thing in my eyes.

I was only in Brixton for four days before it was my big day at the court of appeal. When I was leaving the wing at Brixton everyone was shaking my hand and wishing me luck. I thanked them all as I made my way to the reception area.

The Royal Courts of Justice are where the court of appeals are heard. The Royal Courts are on The Strand in the City of London, along with the Old Bailey and are the most well-known courts in the land. The Guildford 4 and the Birmingham 6 are two of the most infamous cases that were heard there and these cases were serious miscarriages of justice. Who can forget the scenes when Gerry Conlon, one of the Guildford 4, walked out of these courts a free man, after serving fifteen years in prison for a crime he didn't commit?

When I arrived at the courts, I was booked in then placed in a holding cell whilst I waited for my barrister. I was nervous and excited at the same time and when he arrived, we went into a side room where he outlined what would be happening. I was told that there were three possible outcomes. The first was that they could decide that the judge had misled the jury in his summing up and could quash my conviction and sentence and I would be free to go. The second outcome would be that they decided that the judge had misled the jury in his summing up; they could quash my conviction and sentence and request a retrial with a different judge. If this was the result then I would have to apply for bail until the new trial date was arranged. The third and final outcome was that they could decide that the judge hadn't misled the jury and my conviction and sentence would remain. I hadn't thought of the possibility of a retrial but my barrister explained that even though these were the outcomes he thought a retrial was less of a possibility due to the length of time that I had already served.

A clerk of the court came into the room to say that we would be called soon and the barrister wished me luck as we shook hands. I was led up the stairs into the dock and as I looked around, I couldn't believe how old the court looked. You could feel the history seeping out of that room. The other thing I noticed was how quiet the room was. There was only a handful of people in there.

The appeal was underway, dominated by legal jargon between the Crown and my barrister. The case rested on what the judge had thought I said and more importantly had he used this to mislead the jury into finding me guilty. A transcript had been produced of the evidence that I had given at Chester Crown court. In the transcript it clearly stated that I had said, when 'they' were fighting. It was there for all to see and never once had I said when 'we' were fighting, as the judge had gone to great lengths to point out in his summing up. This was the crucial point that my appeal rested on. The Crown commented that the judge had misheard what I said, which would have been all well and good if he hadn't then proceeded to make it the centrepiece of his summing up. My barrister requested that my conviction was now unsafe and I should have my conviction quashed. The Crown said that it had made no difference to my conviction so it should stand.

This could have gone either way. The judges then retired to consult with each other and review the evidence that had been submitted. My barrister came over to me and said that we could do nothing more now except wait. It was down to how much the judge may have influenced the jury.

After what seemed hours the three judges returned with their verdict. The Judge started talking but I could barely hear him from the dock. I was leaning forward, straining to pick up what he was saying and he continued talking for about ten minutes. At this point I thought I heard him say that the original judge had misled the jury but I wasn't sure. He then said the case had been found proven and the judges stood up and walked out of the court room. I didn't know what was happening and I turned to the guard who was in the dock with me and asked him what had happened. He said that I was going home and I turned to my barrister who gave me the thumbs up. I couldn't believe it and I was shacking with adrenaline. The guard led me back down the stairs back into the holding area where my barrister came to see me and we went back into the side room where he explained that the judges had decided that the original judge had totally misled the jury in his summing up. The fact that he had taken what I said and changed it hadn't gone down well at all with the judges. I was absolutely over the moon and thanked my barrister for all his hard work and he wished me well for the future.

That was it I had my conviction and sentence quashed and I was now a free man. A funny thing happened in the holding area, after my barrister left. I went to the desk where the custody officer was and asked me what had happened. He told me that there were some forms to fill in that had to be completed before I could leave and asked me where I was travelling to. I said I was going home to Macclesfield and he said that I would be issued with a travel warrant for my journey home. I was then placed back in the holding cell where there were three men waiting for their hearings. One of them asked me what had happened in court and I told him that I had my conviction quashed and I was going home. He then asked me what I was doing locked in a room if I was free to go home. I laughed but said I didn't know and he told me to get on the bell. I pressed the buzzer and a guard came and opened the cell door. I walked straight past him out of the cell and he asked me what I was doing. I told him that my conviction and sentence had been quashed, I was a free man and that meant I wasn't being locked in that room. He looked at me then told me to wait where I was and started talking to the custody officer. I joined them at the desk and told them that I wasn't being locked up anymore and it was agreed that I would wait in a side room until my as had been processed.

I was in that room for ages until I was issued with my private property. I had all my letters and belongings in a big see-through bag with the words HM Prison Service splatted in big letters on it. I wasn't bothered because I had been issued with a travel warrant and I was on my way home. It felt surreal walking out of the courts and onto The Strand. I turned and looked at the big white building, imagining all the people who had walked out of there, like me a free man. I quietly made a promise to myself that I would never go back to prison and it is a promise that now, twenty-five years later I have kept. I picked up my prison issue bag and made my way to Euston station and the journey home back to my family.

Chapter 17 – A Sweet Smell of Sorrow

When I walked out on to The Strand after having my conviction quashed, I knew that I was done with that way of life. I was sick of having the feeling of dread in the pit of my stomach. The expectation of a knock on the door, early in the morning, after I had got involved in trouble yet again. The endless misery that I had yet again inflicted on my despairing family. Enough was enough. I was 22 years old and I was a dad. I had responsibilities to my daughter that I wanted to fulfil.

When Gaby was born it changed my life, my way of thinking was now different. I had calmed down and I was working and trying to provide for my family, things were changing for the better. I had stopped getting in situations and, for a while, I was staying in. Spending quality time with my family. I had obviously been nicked for the criminal damage on the cars and that was my final warning that I had tried to adhere to. I had convicted and sent to prison which took me away from my family but I had been cleared in the end but I had spent four months away from my family, time I would never get back.

A few days after I had returned home, I met with my solicitor, who I thanked for all her hard work, to apply for compensation for wrongful imprisonment. We filled the forms in, sent the paperwork to the Home Office then waited for the expected pay out that would compensate me for the time away from my family. Unfortunately, I was turned down due to my criminal record. I should have really appealed against this decision and taken it all the way but I didn't because I was young and I was simply happy to be out of there so I left it. I tried again years later but was too late within in the time frames.

I never got any compensation when I was stabbed which was funny really with the amount of compensation that I have paid out over those years.

Since walking out of the Appeal court, I have tried to stay away from getting into trouble. Now I can say that in the past twenty-five years I have managed to do that. I am certainly no angel, absolutely far from it and I have been in my fair share of scrapes since that time. Some of it my doing, a lot of it down to people trying it on with me. Since 1995 I have been in front of the courts just three times and two were for causing a breach of the peace. The other was for assaulting a football referee. I deeply regret what happened. I was totally in the wrong and I offer no excuses. Three times in twenty-five years, with my track record before then, shows that I was serious when I said I was leaving that way of life behind.

It has been a hard road that I have been down, especially when my brother and dad both passed away in tragic circumstances. It would have been easy to press the self-destruct button and then, when I was back in a prison cell, blaming it all on losing my brother and dad but that's the easy option that I never took. The problem is when you are young and you start getting into trouble, you start getting a name, a reputation around the town. This starts off small but the more trouble you get in it starts snowballing, getting bigger until it becomes the thing that I strived for. That is the point where it becomes an avalanche that starts to bury you.

Getting the attention, the reputation that I craved, has cost me dearly. I spent that long trying to be somebody that I really wasn't. I was christened Marc yet everyone knew me as Cozzy. It is like having an alter ego that spiraled out of control. Cozzy wasn't a nice person, in fact he was a bully who didn't care about anyone or anything except being out with his mates doing exactly what he wanted. They say bad publicity is better than no publicity and I craved the attention more than what my family thought of me. My misplaced sense of loyalty to my mates and to the whole environment I regret every day. I regret the heartache, the pain, the tears that I have inflicted on my mum and dad and my brothers and for this I am so sorry. I lost sight of who I actually was and when you spend that long alienating yourself from your family, the closeness that you should share goes forever. I still have my mum and brother Terry who I love very much and I know that they are both there for me as I am for them. The closeness though has gone, dwindled over the years. It's my fault because I should have taken a step back all those years ago, instead of thinking that

I knew it all. I have caused my family a lot of grief and embarrassment over the years but I am lucky that we still have a relationship and for that I am profoundly grateful.

A few years ago, I went around to see my mum with my wife Louise. Gaby my daughter was living at mum's at the time and we were all sat around talking when mum said that she had found a box with some letters that I had written from prison. Louise was reading the letters out loud and everyone was laughing except me. I was totally embarrassed with the content because they were all written in the same vein. All about me, about how I was feeling, about what I needed. Not once did I ask how my family was and not once did I apologise for the pain that I was causing. Listening to these letters horrified me and that night I couldn't sleep. I couldn't stop thinking about how selfish I was and it really affected me. This was the first time that I totally understood the pain and anguish that I had caused my family.

The following morning, I rang my mum and apologised for everything that I had put her through and I listened to her as she told me how I had made my family feel. I was ashamed listening to her and I will regret that for the rest of my life. I apologised to my brother Terry too. He didn't deserve having me as a brother because I never once thought about how my actions would impact him. I was all about me. We shared a bedroom, yet I treated it as if he shouldn't have been there. If Terry spoke up, I would be all over him with my fists, that was my attitude. I know there is still resentment simmering away inside my brother and I know that he can't see that I have changed, that I am not that person anymore.

My behaviour has cost me a lot of relationships over the years. I don't have a relationship with my daughter anymore. She has her issues with me and I understand that. I love Gaby and wish her well. I will always be there for her but I understand that she needs her space.

I have a son Connell who I don't see that much of either he has his issues with me but we have managed to sort them out and I am pleased that we have a relationship. I haven't been a good dad over the years, putting myself before my kids. I have made mistakes with my children for which I hold my hands up. I should have been a better dad. I cannot change the past, all I can do is apologise to Gaby and Connell, it is something that I have to live with and hope that one day we can sort things out.

In writing this book I have tried to work out where I went wrong. I have been in prisons across the country, I have done a lot of things that I am not proud of, I have feelings of regret/ I feel ashamed that my actions have affected others, especially those who are close to me. Looking on exactly have I achieved, the answer is nothing. It has all been a waste of time.

Youngsters today all over the country should read this. There is no happy ending. When you're young you just live for the moment, you don't think of the consequences. You don't think that your actions then, will affect you in years to come. I have spoken about building up your reputation, that's the easy part. The hardest part is losing it and even now it still hangs around my neck like a rusty padlock and chain, it never totally goes away. Even though I am now Marc, Cozzy is always lurking in the shadows ready to spoil the party. The thing that I used to love I have grown to hate with a passion. The fear of getting dragged back into the past embraces my future. I am still feeling the effects from that day in 1989, when I took the blame for what Rob did. I am not putting any blame at Rob's door but that incident trigged the start of a period where I was out of control and when I got charged with the first offence everything changed for me. I see these kids who are heading down the same path and I want to stop them, I want to warn them, that their actions will trigger something and that they won't be able to see or control until it's too late. If one person reads this book and decides to go down another route, that doesn't involve years of regret and heartache it will have been worth writing it. At least some good can come out of this story.

Chapter 18 – And Then There Were Three

The month of September will always have a significant meaning for the Costello family. A big black cloud appears over us, from the beginning of September and stays until the end. It's a hard time for us all, especially my mum. We lost my Grandad Naden on 22nd September 2000 and the following year, on the first anniversary of my Grandad's passing we all attended the cemetery to pay our respects and just a few hours later my brother Danny tragically lost his life aged just twenty.

Danny was at a party at a friend's flat, just enjoying the night like any young lad of his age would. He went out on to the balcony of Sven's tenth floor flat and the next thing they heard was a thud and they looked over and saw Danny on the ground. You can imagine the effect this had on those who were at the flat that night. No one would ever get over what happened that night and it changed so many people's lives.

That night I had been drinking around town and were going to go up to Sven's flat but decided to stay in town drinking instead. I often wonder if I had gone up to Sven's that night, would the outcome have been different. Who knows, maybe or maybe not. I ended going home and falling asleep on the settee and the next thing I know is, I am getting woken up by a lad telling me that there has been an accident involving Danny and we had to go to the police station. I ran all the way there, wondering what the fuck was going on. In hindsight, the lad was doing the right thing by taking me away from the estate. If I had gone up to the flats, God knows what I would have done.

Once we got to the police station, I was informed that Danny had died but they didn't have any more information at that moment in time. I made my way to my mum and dad's house in a daze. I couldn't believe what had happened, I just couldn't believe it. My mum and dad were in bed and my mum came to the door with my dad stood behind and they asked me what was wrong. How do you explain to your parents that their twenty-year old son is dead? I couldn't believe it myself, and mum and dad were devastated. Terry was staying at a house out of town with a few of his mates. I tried ringing him but it kept ringing out. Finally, after ringing one of his mates, I managed to speak to Terry and broke the news. Terry said he was coming straight home and the rest of the morning is a blur.

The police came to my mum's along with a family liaison officer. Terry arrived home devastated as you can imagine and this was the start of a living nightmare for us all. The shock of losing a brother is something that you can't really describe. The fact that everyone knew him meant there was a lot of people grieving for Danny.

Danny was my younger brother; he was a lot closer to Terry due to the fact they lived together at my mum and dads. They also enjoyed DJing together, something which they were both really into. When I was getting in to all the trouble Danny was nine-years old which meant I wasn't there for him as I should have been.

As Danny got a bit older, he started getting into his fair share of trouble and would not settle at school, he would just walk out. My mum tried everything to get him to go but nothing worked and, in the end, Danny ended up in a residential school in Ellesmere Port. That was until he walked out of there and made his way home.

He did the same when he started his scaffolding apprenticeship, part of the course meant that they had to go to an outward-bound centre in Snowdonia in north Wales. One day they got to the bottom of Snowdonia, when they were informed that they were climbing it that day. Danny just turned around and told the instructor that he wasn't doing it. The instructor told him that he had to, otherwise he would fail the course. Danny still refused, arguing that it had nothing to do with scaffolding. In the end Danny just walked off back down the mountain, all the way to the nearest train station where he jumped on the first train that pulled in and made his way home. He never did climb that mountain.

Danny was a handful at times and the fact that he was my brother did him no favours whereas Terry has never been in trouble in his life. My reputation meant that Danny was always in my shadow and he had my reputation to live up to. I wish I had sat down with Danny and told him that it wasn't worth it but I doubt he would have listened to me.

In 2021 it will be twenty years since Danny passed away and it still feels like it was only yesterday. I sit and wonder what he might have become. Would we have worked together? Would he have had his own little family? Who knows what he would have gone on to achieve? Danny's death changed the family in more ways than you can imagine and I think that day has affected us all long term.

Four years later, a week after his anniversary on the 30th September 2015, my dad took his own life. My Dad had his battles with mental health over the years, along with his constant health problems and he had obviously decided enough was enough. My Dad changed a lot over the years and he had become hard to live with. I didn't see much of this because again, I was caught up in my own life. Looking back, when I called round, everything seemed fine and to me that meant everything was good when clearly it wasn't. My mum and dad eventually separated and finally divorced. Dad was living on his own when he was found dead. It's only when I got older that I realised that my dad just wanted the best for me. The one thing that I always remember about my dad was that he was well known and well respected as a hard worker in the scaffolding business. He would proudly introduce me to his work colleagues as his son and that used to make me feel like I was on top of the world.

Working together made us become close and it made me understand what my dad was about. He was a hardworking man who wanted the best for his family. Dad used to thumb a lift to Manchester and then back just to get a day's money to provide for his family. That was just how he was; family came first. Things started going wrong for dad when he started getting bad chest infections. He would get rid of one, then soon after he would get another. Dad was in and out of hospital then the doctor announced that he wasn't fit for work and he had to retire due to ill health. This was a massive blow to him as dad used to work twelve hours a day, seven days a week and over a period of time he started getting depressed. I don't think he could handle never working again. He was in his forties when he had to stop working and then one night tried to kill himself. This attempt failed, resulting in him been starved of oxygen to his brain and I think is where his issues with mental health started.

Unfortunately, he would suffer from this, until he couldn't take it anymore. When you lose your brother and ad in tragic circumstances, it affects you for the rest of your life. You think you are alright but it changes you as a person, it tears you in half at times. I have a lot of guilt that I carry around with me. I should have been the big brother and made time and effort to be there for him and it's the same for all my family. I have let them down all down and this eats away at me especially now that I am older. I cannot change the past, that has been and gone but am sorry for everything that I put my family through and for not being a good dad to Gaby and Connell. That is why I wanted to write this book to draw a line under the past and look to the future. I am not the person that you read about in this book anymore.

I am Marc Costello. Two very different people, in two very different places.

There is nothing glamorous about this story and there is no happy ending. It is a book about regrets. It is about guilt. It is about ruined relationships. It's an apology to everyone that I have hurt.

If you are a young person knocking about in the wrong crowd, trying to impress your mates, doing stupid things, making stupid decisions. If you are fighting with your parents thinking you know it all then please read this book. What happened to me could happen to you and ask yourself is it worth it in the long run? I can say to you that the answer is no. Do your own thing, walk your own path. The future is anything you want it to be. It's your life so live it the best way you can.

Epilogue

I have been thinking about writing this book for many years. I never had the time or confidence to actually get around to putting pen to paper but I have had a title for my book for about twenty years. I started thinking seriously about writing when I started listening to podcasts. I would listen to these guys telling fascinating stories about their lives. Their experiences they had both in and out of prison and this got me thinking that maybe I had a story to tell after all. I sat down and talked to my wife Louise about it and she thought this was a great idea. I spoke to my mum and then to my brother Terry to see what they thought and I don't think they believed I would actually go through with it.

When the country went into lockdown, I decided that I now had time on my hands, so I would start writing. What I didn't realise when I started was how hard it would be mentally. In parts I have had to go into myself and dig deep, bringing back incidents that I had long since buried. I have had to face up to my past and face the consequences of my actions. The pain that I have inflicted on my family, well that has been hard. Now I can finally put my past into a box, close the lid and move on.

I am lucky. I survived and I came out of it to the other side. I am happily married to my rock and best friend Louise. I have a stepson Tom who is a good lad. Meeting my wife means that I gained another family who are always there for me as well. I am finally settled at long last; I feel comfortable with who I am and with my role in life and I thank my beautiful wife for that.

We, as a family, have been through our fair share of tragedy. We have come through and it has made us stronger. It's been a long road with plenty of ups and downs but one thing I have learned through this is that everyone makes mistakes in life. It doesn't mean they have to pay for them for the rest of their lives though. Sometimes good people make bad choices. It doesn't make them bad; it means they are human.

Family is what is important, your mates will come and go. They will let you down but your family will always be there for you. For that fact, I am forever grateful.

The End

Printed by Amazon Italia Logistica S.r.l.
Torrazza Piemonte (TO), Italy